Also by Kevin Barrett:

Dr. Weirde's Weirde Tours:
A Guide to Mysterious
San Francisco
(San Francisco, CA: Last Gasp, 1994)

Truth Jihad
(Joshua Tree, CA: Progressive Press, 2007)

Edited with John Cobb and Sandra Lubarsky:
9/11 & American Empire v2: Christians,
Jews, & Muslims Speak Out
(Northampton, MA: Interlink, 2007)

Questioning the War on Terror:

A Primer for Obama Voters

By Kevin Barrett

Khadir Press

KHADIR PRESS
Madison, WI

All inquiries:
khadirpress@gmail.com

Mailing address for orders and correspondence:
P.O. Box 221
Lone Rock, WI 53556

This book is published by Khidria, Inc., a registered 501C3 nonprofit
corporation, for educational purposes. Those wishing to help distribute
this book for educational purposes may purchase quantities of ten for
fifty dollars plus five dollars postage (within the U.S.A.) by sending
a check or money order for $55 to: Khidria, Inc., P.O. Box 221, Lone
Rock, WI 53556.

Cover design by Sandra Taylor, The Graphic Page

Manufactured in the United States of America

ISBN 978-1-4276-4138-0

Preface: Two Big Questions

Part One: In Which Your Humble Author Questions Whether All This Is Really Necessary

Part Two: Case Studies in Questionable Terrorism

In memory of my late aunt, Mary Goulding, an Obama fan whose questioning spirit informs these pages, and whose enthusiastic encouragement helped inspire and sustain the writing of this book, which she did not quite live long enough to read.

I would also like to thank Sachi Kuhananthan, M.D. and Peter Kogen, who helped inspire and develop this book; my wife and children, in love and gratitude; and the many others who contributed ideas, time, money, conversation, and patience.

–Kevin Barrett, www.truthjihad.com

"Barack Obama will confront a daunting list of priorities when he takes office on Jan. 20. Rescuing the nation's economy—if there's anything left to rescue by then—will obviously be at the top of the list. But it is just as important that Obama immediately declare an end to the 'war on terror,' and reverse all of the policies that have been carried out in its name."

– Gary Kamiya, "Why Obama should end the 'war on terror': Bush's infantile response to 9/11 has harmed our national interests for too long. It's time to declare it dead."
– Salon.com, Nov. 25, 2008.

"A deliberate strategy to misrepresent 9/11 to sell a war against a country that had nothing to do with 9/11."

– Barack Obama

"Using bold rhetoric that often makes his followers rapturous, Barack Obama has declared over and over that he will be the president of 'change.' But is Obama brave enough to bring about a really radical change? Will he end the permanent 'war' George W. Bush has left us with? Will a candidate or a President Obama be willing to go so far as to question whether 'the war on terror'— the framework for nearly every discussion of U.S. foreign policy today—is truly the pre-eminent challenge of our time?"

– Michael Hirsh, "Memo to President Obama: Never mind Iraq. Just end the 'war on terror.'"
– Newsweek, February 21st, 2008.

"Thanks to the 9/11 Commission, we know that six years ago this week President Bush received a briefing with the headline: 'Bin Ladin determined to strike in U.S.'"

– Barack Obama

"It is perhaps a paradox—and one that is fitting for the strangeness of our current age—that we will need to end the war against terrorism because we cannot end terrorism."

– Princeton scholar G. John Ikenberry

"We did not reaffirm our basic values, or secure our homeland. Instead, we got a color-coded politics of fear."

– Barack Obama

"The next administration needs to do better. The place to begin is with the candid recognition that the Global War on Terror has effectively ceased to exist."

– Andrew J. Bacevich, professor of history and international relations at Boston University, "Expanding War, Contracting Meaning: The Next President and the Global War on Terror." The Philadelphia Jewish Voice #41, December 2008.

"In the dark halls of Abu Ghraib and the detention cells of Guantanamo, we have compromised our most precious values."

– Barack Obama

"The U.S. government has consistently blamed me for being behind every occasion its enemies attack it. I would like to assure the world that I did not plan the recent attacks, which seem to have been planned by people for personal reasons."

– Osama Bin Laden, quoted by CNN, September 17th, 2001

"It is time to turn the page. It is time to write a new chapter in our response to 9/11."

– Barack Obama

Osama Bin Laden is "not wanted" for 9/11 because there is "no hard evidence" against him.

– FBI spokesperson Rex Tomb, stating official FBI position on Bin Laden and 9/11

"I am aware that some question or justify the events of 9/11. But let us be clear: al-Qaeda killed nearly 3,000 people on that day. The victims were innocent men, women and children from America and many other nations who had done nothing to harm anybody. And yet al-Qaeda chose to ruthlessly murder these people, claimed credit for the attack, and even now states their determination to kill on a massive scale. . . . These are not opinions to be debated; these are facts to be dealt with."

– President Barack Obama, Cairo speech, June 4th 2009.

"I have already said that I am not involved in the 11 September attacks in the United States. As a Muslim, I try my best to avoid telling a lie. I had no knowledge of these attacks, nor do I consider the killing of innocent women, children and other humans as an appreciable act. "

– Osama Bin Laden, quoted in *Ummat* (Karachi, Pakistan) September 28th, 2001

"As the Holy Koran tells us, 'Be conscious of God and speak always the truth.'"

– President Barack Obama, Cairo speech, June 4th 2009.

Preface: Two Big Questions

First Question:
Is This the End of Bush's Reign of Terror?

The election of Barack Hussein Obama tacked a giant flashing neon question mark onto the Bush Administration's much-ballyhooed but never clearly defined "War on Terror." Surveys showed that McCain voters, like Bush voters before them, were heavily motivated by fear of terrorists. Obama voters, on the other hand, were more worried about the economy.

By voting for a dark-skinned guy with a Muslim father, a middle name Hussein and a last name that sounds like Osama, Americans were saying they didn't buy the Fox News propaganda demonizing Arabs, Muslims, and other vaguely dark-skinned people with funny names.

By voting for the man they perceived as the anti-war candidate, Americans were re-stating the message they had sent in 2006: End the war NOW already! (What is it about the word NOW that the politicians don't understand?)

Americans turned against the war when they learned that it had been based on lies. Bush lied when he claimed Saddam Hussein posed a threat to America. He lied when he said Saddam had weapons of mass destruction. He lied when he said the war in Iraq was about WMD not oil, and the war in Afghanistan was about terror not a gas pipeline. In handing the Republicans yet another crushing electoral defeat, American voters were saying they didn't buy Bush's lies any more.

The rejection of the Republicans was also a rejection of torture. Obama campaigned for ending torture and closing Guantanamo, and the voters responded enthusiastically.

Obama's election showed the voters sensed a close connection between Bush's hugely expensive, ruinous War on Terror and the economic difficulties America is facing. By running up a ten trillion dollar deficit and dragging America's good name through the mud, Bush had wrecked the economy. Perhaps Obama, the peace candidate whose top priority was the economy, would be able to fix it.

For all of the above reasons, Obama's victory made it okay to question the so-called War on Terror. Asking the hard questions is no longer heretical, as it was during the darkest days of the reign of Bad King George.

Maybe it's even time to ask some hard questions about Obama, as Webster Tarpley does in *Obama: The Unauthorized Biography*. Voters who were expecting Obama to end the War on Terror have been discomfited by some of his early decisions:

• In March 2009, Obama announced yet another escalation of the war in Afghanistan, suggesting it would be expanded into Pakistan: "On top of the 17,000 additional US troops Obama has already deployed to Afghanistan, he announced plans to send 4,000 more."[1] By attacking the sovereign nation of Pakistan, which has neither attacked nor threatened the U.S., Obama appeared to be extending Bush's policy of repeatedly committing the supreme war crime, aggression. And by targeting civilians in Pakistan, Obama appeared to be condoning secondary war crimes as well.[2] In April 2009, Secretary of Defense Robert Gates, a holdover from the Bush Administration, told Voice of America "that the United States was preparing to fight 'irregular wars' across the Muslim world for years to come." The same VOA report quoted the US Joint Forces Command "saying that the United States was prepared to confront insurgencies and small-scale threats (across the Muslim world) for the next 25 years." While 25 years of war is not the new 100 years' war McCain promised, neither is it the peace Obama voters expected.[3] Is Obama really personally committed to this agenda? Or is he simply unable to paddle against the flood of militarism unleashed by the Bush Administration's War on Terror? If enough Americans questioned the War on Terror, would Obama change course? Could President Obama still become the peace president we thought we were voting for?

• While claiming to be withdrawing combat troops from Iraq, Obama's military will be keeping more than 10,000 combat troops in Baghdad alone—indefinitely—"in the guise of trainers and advisers in what are effectively combat roles."[4] The total number of official U.S. troops in Iraq will remain at about 50,000.[5] They will continue to carry out "targeted counterterrorism missions," a euphemism for murdering Iraqis brave enough to fight for the independence of their country.[6] The cost of this continued occupation will be enormous—half a million dollars per year for each sergeant according to a Senate inquiry.[7] In addition to those 50,000 troops, "there is almost a parallel army of American mercenaries and private military contractors whose numbers range from 100,000 to 150,000" who are not leaving.[8] If his supporters demand the complete U.S. withdrawal from Iraq they voted for in 2006 and again in 2008, would Obama resist their wishes? Might he actually be happy if it became politically feasible to do the right thing?

• According to the April 17th 2009 U.K. *Independent*, "Barack Obama yesterday confirmed he will shield from prosecution CIA operatives who inflicted waterboarding and other extreme interrogation techniques against terror suspects during the Bush years, even as the White House released memos containing shocking new details of what was permitted in their secret prisons."[9] Torture tactics described in these memos included the use of insects to torture innocent children.[10] A Red Cross report states that CIA medical personnel monitored the torture sessions, just as the Nazi doctors did under the Third Reich.[11] Reports that suppressed Abu Ghaib photos show rape, murder, and worse were confirmed by mainstream sources, while according to former National Security Agency officer Wayne Madsen, "the orders to take the sexually-oriented photos and videos, some of which involve teenage Iraqi boys and girls and sodomization by their guards, came directly from a pedophile and closeted male homosexual ring operating in the White House, according to the intelligence sources. Copies of the tapes and photos were sent directly to the White House for the entertainment of senior members of the Bush White House, including officials in the Vice President's office and the Executive Office of the President." Madsen adds that ""installation of live streaming black boxes in the White House and the Eisenhower Old Executive Office Building used to stream live video of torture sessions in Guantanamo, Cuba and Abu Ghraib to the Old Executive Office Building office of Vice President Dick Cheney's Chief Counsel David Addington and into the White House, itself. Media reports of torture sessions being taped may have been planted by the White House to deter investigators away from

15

looking at live streaming capabilities in the offices of Cheney and President Bush."[12]

Despite his announced intention to shield torturers from prosecution, Obama's decision to release Bush Administration torture memos suggests that he actually wouldn't mind seeing the high-level torture culprits investigated and prosecuted. After all, Obama has ordered Guantanamo closed and repudiated torture in the strongest terms. He must have known that releasing those documents would generate a groundswell of outrage that could lead to prosecutions. He may even be quietly hoping that his supporters rise up and demand a torture investigation, which could lead to prosecutions of other Bush Administration crimes related to the "War on Terror." Perhaps Obama hopes his base is smart enough to see that by demanding prosecutions of Bush Administration crimes—prosecutions that can only happen if millions of people demand them—it will not only be good for America, but also good for the Democrats in the 2010 midterm elections.

• According to Glen Greenwald, Obama's Justice Department has outdone even Bush in defending Bush's illegal spying and kidnapping programs against the American judicial system:

"In the last week alone, the Obama DOJ (a) attempted to shield Bush's illegal spying programs from judicial review by (yet again) invoking the very 'state secrets' argument that Democrats spent years condemning and by inventing a brand new 'sovereign immunity' claim that not even the Bush administration espoused, and (b) argued that individuals abducted outside of Afghanistan by the U.S. and then 'rendered' to and imprisoned in Bagram have no rights of any kind—not even to have a hearing to contest the accusations against them—even if they are not Afghans and were captured far away from any 'battlefield.' These were merely the latest—and among the most disturbing—in a string of episodes in which the Obama administration has explicitly claimed to possess the very presidential powers that Bush critics spent years condemning as radical, lawless and authoritarian."[13] Does Obama really seek unconstitutional presidential powers? Or is he the captive of a larger transformation of the division of power designed by Dick Cheney and the neoconservatives and pushed through using the shock effect of 9/11 and the War on Terror? Would President

16

Obama happily relinquish those powers if enough Americans rose up and demanded a return to constitutional governance?

• Despite getting elected as a peace candidate, Obama asked for and received a massive 20-billion-dollar (4%) hike in the military budget—a budget that had doubled during the Bush years due to the War on Terror.[14] Does Obama really support bloated military budgets? Or is he a prisoner of the War on Terror paradigm designed by the previous administration?

This book sets out to ask the hard questions about the "War on Terror." If enough Obama voters ask these hard questions loudly enough, they will get the change they voted for. If they don't, they won't. It really is that simple.

Second Big Question: Did the War on Terror Trigger Economic Collapse?

According to a 2007 estimate by CNNmoney.com, "the 'War on Terror' may cost $2.4 trillion."[15] Then in 2008, *Bloomberg* conveyed an even more frightening figure from Nobel laureate Alfred Stiglitz: "Economist Stiglitz Says Iraq War Costs May Reach $5 Trillion."[16]

If the Iraq war alone tops $5 trillion, even as troops continue to surge into the Afghanistan quagmire, the total cost of the War on Terror might turn out to be...what...$10 trillion? And if this war does not end in our lifetime, are we looking at $20 trillion? $50 trillion? Perhaps even $100 trillion?

By comparison, the entire gross domestic product (GDP) of the United States is less than $15 trillion.

$2.4 trillion here...$5 trillion there...pretty soon you're talking about real money.

Is it purely coincidental that after 50 years of robust growth, the U.S. economy started slowing down in late 2001, and has been adrift in worsening doldrums ever since? Has the War on Terror actually been a war on the economy?

The War on Terror has doubled military spending.[17] And economists have shown that of all forms of government spending, military spending is the most economically destructive.[18] The reasons are not difficult to understand. Military spending creates nothing. In fact, it is worse than useless. It amounts to paying people to destroy property and lives. And when we spend vast amounts of money training large numbers of people to become professional destroyers of property and lives, what we get in return is not just a big fat zero, but an actual drain on our society and our economy.

When the government spends money on schools, it creates a better-educated, therefore more economically productive, population. When it spends money on roads and bridges, it gets a more economically productive infrastructure. When it spends money on research geared toward better meeting basic human needs such as food, energy, housing, transportation, and medical care, it invests in potentially huge payoffs. If it pays artists to produce art and do art education, it stimulates the whole society's creativity. And if it just pays people to dig holes in the ground and fill them back up with dirt, at least it does no harm.

But when the government pays people to develop bombs and missiles and warheads whose purpose is to blow up valuable objects created at immense expense of human time and labor, and to kill large numbers of human beings, each with his or her own set of skills and his or her own creative, productive potential, it is not only doing no good, but actually wreaking immense harm. Increasingly, researchers are discovering that grave harm is done not only to the people who are killed, and whose property is destroyed, but also to those who are trained to be the killers and destroyers.

The simple truth is that the military trains young human beings to be murderers. It should therefore be no surprise that "murder, crime and military spending are 99.6% proportional internationally among the leading industrial nations."[19] The young Pentagon-trained murderers pay the price—with the loss of their own souls—while the society around them also pays the price, as domestic murder and crime rates skyrocket right along with military spending.

The US, which spends more military money than all the other major powers combined, also spends far more money on prisons. With only five percent of the world's population, the US cages almost a quarter of the world's prisoners. Torture is rampant throughout the U.S. prison system.[20] As military spending pushes crime rates through the roof, society has to spend vast amounts of money hiring police and judges and court officials and prison guards, building prisons, and treating victims, who, like tortured prisoners, become less economically productive due to the trauma they suffer. In all likelihood, the whole population of a gulag society becomes less productive as its energy switches from exuberant, fearless creativity to craven timidity.

Another way the War on Terror has damaged the economy has been widely noted: America's good name has been sullied, and its reputation in the world flushed down the toilet. Polls have discovered that Europeans consider the United States of America, not Iran or North Korea, the biggest threat to global peace.[21] And the rest of the world thinks even less of the U.S. than the Europeans do.

The War on Terror has destroyed international confidence in America's stability, if not its sanity, undermining the willingness of foreign investors to keep propping up the U.S. economy in the face of ever-growing deficits caused by excessive U.S. military spending. As foreign investors pull out of the U.S. economy, a Great Depression style catastrophe looms on the horizon. Investors have been nervously watching China in anticipation of its decision to stop propping up the US dollar—a decision that would wreak economic havoc.[22]

In the face of an uncertain economic future, one thing is clear: By triggering what are euphemistically called "wars of choice" or "discretionary wars" or "pre-emptive wars"—which might be more accurately called "pointless, illegal wars" or "mass murder for the hell of it"—the War on Terror has inflicted grave economic damage on the U.S.A. The only questions are how grave, and where does it end.

Introduction: "Is All This Really Necessary?"

Not so very long ago, I rushed to the Phoenix airport early on a mid-winter Monday morning, only to discover that there was no way in hell I was going to make my plane. The TSA checkpoint line was a giant cattle pen overflowing with nervous bovine humanoids lowing grumpily en route to inevitable slaughter. There were thousands of them. Each one would have to remove shoes, belt, watch, jewelry and other metallic items, place all of his or her belongings in little plastic trays alongside laptops and carry-ons, walk through a scanner, recover the belongings, put on shoes, watch, belt, watch, and jewelry, and move along.

I was heading home by way of Chicago, where a blizzard had dumped a foot of snow, disrupting air traffic and creating a major passenger backlog. I thought to myself: "By the time I got through this line, I will have not only missed my flight, but the next two or three flights as well. I will be put at the end of a very long list of passengers waiting for a seat to open up on a future flight. This is not fun."

An artificially menacing voice on the PA system informed me that the terror threat level had been raised to orange. Since 9/11, it seemed to be permanently stuck on orange. Why did they keep saying it had just been raised? It hadn't been raised or lowered for years. Did they really think Americans had so little sense of history, such complete lack of memory of what had gone before, that the authorities could keep right on scaring us by implying that the terror threat had just been raised to orange?

Of course they did.

After what felt like interminable hours of boredom, the passage of time marked by the number of "terror threat has been raised to orange" announcements on the PA, a starched-shirted TSA man wandered out to our part of the cattle pen to advise us about what to do if and when we should ever reach the security checkpoint. After going through a complicated set of instructions concerning such things as how many ounces of liquid or gel could be carried in what sort of container, he finished with "Are there any questions?" This was my chance. "Yes, I have a question. Since terrorism is not a statistically significant threat, and since we still haven't had a real investigation of 9/11...is all of this REALLY necessary?" After a long moment of silence, with all heads turned, the TSA man recovered with "Let me re-phrase that...are there any *intelligent* questions?" A couple of passengers tittered. "Yes, there are—a whole bunch of them," I began...but by then the TSA man had turned his back on us, intent on informing another corner of the cattle pen just how much liquid or gel could be carried in which kind of containers.

After hours spent getting through the checkpoint line and to the gate, I discovered that I had indeed missed my plane. I was indeed

20

put at the end of a long list of stand-by passengers. I did indeed spend the whole day at the Phoenix Airport waiting for a seat to open up on a flight to Chicago, listening to the threat advisory being endlessly raised to orange. Late that night I finally got on a flight to Chicago, where I spent the night with a few hundred other stranded passengers in a blocked-off wing of the airport, on military-style folding cots. It took most of the next day to get home from Chicago by way of St. Louis. The threat level always remained "raised to orange."

During that long trip home, I kept thinking of the TSA man saying "Are there any questions?" The more I thought about it, the more questions I had.

This book is co-dedicated to that devoted public servant, the starch-shirted TSA man at the Phoenix airport who asked me if there were any questions.

Part One:
In Which Your Humble Author Questions Whether All This Is Really Necessary

Is Terrorism Really a Significant Threat?

Statistically, there are good grounds for wondering whether we should bother to worry about terrorism at all. Roughly 3,000 Americans have been killed by terrorists during the past century. In other words, a whole century's worth of terror victims equals three days' worth of cigarette fatalities, a week's worth of deaths from bad medical treatment, or a month's worth of automobile deaths.[23] Shouldn't we worry far more about cigarettes, doctors, and automobiles than about terrorists?

And how does your chance of being killed by terrorists compare with your chance of being struck by lighting? It turns out that lighting is a vastly greater threat. There are, on average, about 1,000 lightning victims per year in the USA, whereas the average number of terror victims per year—a number wildly skewed upward by the fluke of 9/11—is still only about thirty.[24]

Are terrorists at least more dangerous than...bathtubs? Nope. It turns out that your chances of drowning in your bathtub are more than ten times as great as your chances of being killed by a terrorist.[25]

Should we declare war against lightning bolts and bathtubs? Should we install PA systems in our bathrooms reminding us that the threat level of bathtub drowning has been raised to orange? Should we create a new Department of Bathtub Security (DBS) empowered to do sneak-and-peak warrantless searches of our bathrooms to make sure that we're using no-slip bath-mats? Should we invade and occupy countries that we falsely blame for bathtub deaths? Would this be any crazier than what we're doing now, allegedly due to the equally insignificant "terrorist threat"?

Do We Really Need Security Checkpoints at Airports?

In the 1960s, airplane hijackings were common, and passengers on hijacked planes sometimes got killed. Still there were no security checkpoints. You could arrive at the airport at 12:55 for a 1 pm flight, sprint through the airport, and have a chance of catching the plane. I actually did this once or twice in the late 1970s.

Are things really so much worse now, hijacking-wise, that we have to make air travel such a miserable experience? If we eliminated all airport security tomorrow, just how big a risk would we be courting? Since air travel is vastly safer than automobile travel, wouldn't you still be more likely to suffer death or injury from an automobile accident en route to the airport than to become a terror casualty? If so, is it really a good idea to make air travel marginally safer, and infinitely less pleasant, by turning airports into miniature police states?

Are There Really "People Out There Who Want to Kill Us" Who Pose a Catastrophic Threat?

We're told that the threat advisory is always being raised to orange because "there are people out there who want to kill us." But are there really significant numbers of well-organized, competent people who want to kill Americans in big terrorist attacks? Who exactly are these people, what precisely do they want, and why do they think big terrorist attacks on American civilians will help them achieve their goals? Why would Arab and Muslim militants, who want the U.S. and especially Israel out of the Middle East, think that launching terrorist attacks on American civilians could somehow help their cause? Attacks against Israel, of course, might make sense to Arab and Muslim militants, because those attacks damage Israel's fragile, tourism-dependent economy and cause decreased Jewish immigration to Israel, and increased Jewish emigration from Israel, which could eventually lead to the Palestinians reclaiming their lost homeland.

But why would Arab and Muslim militants want to attack the U.S.A.? Big, spectacular terrorist attacks in the U.S.A. are guaranteed to rally the American people against the (alleged) perpetrators. Such attacks obviously would not get the U.S. out of the Middle East nor end U.S. support for Israel; instead, they would be perfectly tailored for getting the U.S. deeper into the Middle East and increasing U.S. support for Israel.

Were the Vietnamese stupid enough to think that blowing up American skyscrapers would get the U.S. out of Vietnam? Of course not. Are Arabs and Muslims that much stupider than the Vietnamese? Not likely. So is there any reason to think than any Arab and Muslim militants smart enough to pull off big terrorist acts in the U.S.A. would even want to?

Are Muslim Extremists Prone to Suicide Terrorism?

First, what exactly do we mean by "extremists"? If we are talking about Muslims who demonstrate in the streets, burning U.S. flags and chanting "yankee go home," such people are (1) no more numerous in Muslim countries than in non-Muslim countries, and (2) not especially likely to have strong religious commitments. These people are anti-imperialists and anti-colonialists, whether they pray five times a day or not, whether they believe in God or not.

Are anti-imperialists and anti-colonialists who happen to be Muslim more likely to commit suicide terrorism than non-Muslims of the same political orientation? According to the best research, the answer is no. Robert Pape is a University of Chicago professor who wrote *Dying to Win: The Strategic Logic of Suicide Terrorism*. Pape's exhaustive study of every suicide attack between 1980 and

2003 concludes: "The data show that there is little connection between suicide terrorism and Islamic fundamentalism, or any one of the world's religions."[26] Instead, people of any or no religion use suicide terrorism as a weapon of last resort when their lands are invaded and occupied.

But What About the Palestinians and Iraqis Blowing Themselves Up? Aren't They Motivated by Islamic Visions of Paradise?

If Americans can be motivated to die for their country by visions of fluttering flags and Memorial Day parades and belief in the Christian heaven, why shouldn't Palestinians and Iraqis be motivated to die for THEIR countries by celebrations of fallen heroes and belief in Islam's vision of paradise? But Palestinians and Iraqis are not the world champion suicide terrorists. That honor falls to the Tamil Tigers, a secularist Hindu group.[27] The Tamil Tigers are motivated by the same kinds of cultural forces that convince people to die for their countries in the U.S.A., in Palestine, in Iraq, and everywhere else.

What Exactly IS Terrorism, Anyway?[28]

The words "terrorism" and "terrorist" are insults that almost anyone can use against almost any enemy. Our soldiers are heroes; their soldiers are terrorists. To an Iraqi or Afghani, a roadside bomber targeting a U.S. convoy is a soldier and a hero, while the U.S. occupying forces are terrorists. To U.S. troops, on the other hand, any native who resists U.S. occupation is a terrorist. But polls have shown that most Iraqis support attacks on U.S. troops.[29] So it's clear that the U.S. troops' definition of terrorism is a minority view in Iraq. In Afghanistan a poll by Western public opinion specialists, whose bias against the resistance is obvious, found that one-fourth of the population supports attacks on U.S. troops, and that this support is growing rapidly as of 2009.[30] That poll probably understates the real feeling of Afghanis, who, like all other peoples, do not want to live under foreign occupation.

The self-styled Department for Jewish Zionist Education offers this definition of terrorism: "Situations deliberately directed against civilians or military in non-military Acts (sic) of murder and destruction."[31] But what, exactly, is a "non-military act"? When Israeli snipers deliberately murder hundreds of Palestinian children in schoolyards and streets, is that a "military act" because the child-killers are in uniform?[32] Obviously whether you consider any particular act of violence a legitimate military act, or an illegitimate act of "non-military" terrorism, depends on your point of view. From a Palestinian point of view, the military wing of Hamas may be the most legitimate military organization in Palestine/Israel—they did win in free and fair elections, after all—while the IDF is a gang of terrorists. From an Israeli viewpoint, the roles are reversed.

Is it possible to define terrorism in a way that applies equally to everybody? Wikipedia has offered the following definition: "Violence against civilians to achieve political or ideological objectives by creating fear." But since all modern wars feature widespread "violence against civilians to achieve political or ideological objectives by creating fear," that means war *is* terrorism. Wars that involve invading and occupying another country, in particular, are terrorist enterprises. People always resist when foreigners invade and occupy their lands. In occupied lands, virtually everyone supports the resistance, so there is no clear distinction between civilians and soldiers within the occupied population. Anti-occupation struggles consist of native civilians struggling against an occupying foreign military. The only way the occupiers can attempt to put down the resistance is to use violence against those civilians in order to inspire fear. The most brutal and bloody terrorist episodes in history, then, are invasions and occupations, such as the Nazi invasion and occupation of Europe, the French invasion and occupation of Algeria, the Zionist invasion and occupation of Palestine, and the U.S. invasions and occupations of Vietnam, Afghanistan, and Iraq. These terrorist acts, taken together, have killed tens of millions.

But wait! Don't the corporate media mainly use the word "terrorist" to describe civilians living under (terrorist) occupation who are fighting to resist the (terrorist) occupiers? And isn't this an Orwellian use of language? Is war really peace? Is freedom really slavery? Is ignorance really strength? And are civilians who are being terrorized by terrorist invasions and occupations, and who resist the terrorist occupiers, really the terrorists?

Whichever side you sympathize with, it's obvious that war has become the only significant form of terrorism on earth, and governments the only significant terrorists. As we have seen, non-uniformed insurgents—the kind of people the corporate media labels "terrorists"—pose less of a threat to U.S. civilians than lightning strikes and bathtub drownings. On the other hand, governments and their militaries kill millions of civilians, and it gets worse all the time. Allen Roland writes:

> In the First World War 5 per cent of those killed were civilians, in the Second World War 48 per cent, while in a Third World War 90-95 per cent would be civilians. We are already seeing those percentages reached in America's illegal war and occupation of Iraq, where over a million Iraqis have been killed and displaced, and also in Israel's recent illegal assault of Gaza where over 1400 Palestinian civilians have been slaughtered.[33]

Is the War on Terror a PR blitz by the world's only significant terrorists—governments—to convince us to support their terrorism?

Is War on Terror the Right Metaphor?

There are some events that all of us can agree to describe as wars. World War I and World War II, for example, featured large numbers of men dressing up in uniform and going at it with guns and bombs of various sizes. The United States Congress declared war. There is no question that these events were wars.

But after World War II, the U.S. armed forces got heavily involved in places like Korea and Vietnam and Iraq even though Congress never declared war against those countries. Again, large numbers of people were dressing in uniform and engaging in mass killing. But as far as Congress and the Constitution were concerned, these weren't wars.

Still, we refer to "the Korean war and "the Vietnam war" and "Gulf War One" and so on. Deep down inside, we know it is crazy to claim these were not wars.

So we have a pretty good idea of what a literal war really is. But what about the "war on drugs?" That, of course, is a metaphor. When we use this expression, we know we are not talking about a bunch of soldiers shooting it out with an army of mind-altering substances. But doesn't that image color the way we think about drugs and drug policy?

Likewise with the "War on Terror." How can you fight a war against an abstract noun?

Terror means "extreme fear." How can you fight a war against extreme fear? Can you kill fear? Force it to surrender? Negotiate with it? Convince it to sign a peace treaty?

Can a war against extreme fear ever end?

Could we end it just by realizing that we're using the wrong metaphor?

Is the War on Terror a Scam?

Just where did this wacky War on Terror metaphor come from, anyway? Who thought it up? Who benefits from it? Might there be a connection between the people who thought it up and disseminated it, and those who gain materially and financially from it?

The war-on-terror metaphor became a dominant paradigm shortly after 9/11. The Cheney-Bush administration could have called the attack what it was—a crime. It was obviously a mass murder, an act of willful destruction of property, maybe even insurance fraud.

But the Cheney-Bush administration showed no interest in solving the crime of 9/11, or even acknowledging that it *was* a crime. Instead, they framed it as an act of war by "international terrorists." The response would be to ignore the crime of 9/11, make no effort whatsoever to investigate the crime, and instead declare an endless "War on Terror." By claiming the nation was at war, Cheney and Bush could seize near-absolute power and crack down on dissent. They and their cronies could rake in billions of dollars in military and homeland security contracts. They could use U.S. military and police forces pretty much any way they wanted to. In short, they used the idea of a War on Terror to grab oodles of money and near-absolute power.

The *Dallas Morning News* found that in Texas, homeland security money was being spent on traffic stops, drug investigations, and community festivals. And an audit by the Texas Engineering Extension Office discovered that homeland security money was being spent on lawn mower drag races.[34] In Wisconsin, DHS money has paid for clown and puppet shows. A congressional investigation found many other similar outrages, including homeland security money for mushroom festivals, bulletproof vests for police dogs, and dozens of security cameras for remote Alaskan fishing villages.[35] Is this a sensible use of taxpayers' money?

Could the whole War on Terror metaphor be a gigantic scam?

America's War on Terror—Or Israel's?

Most Americans think the War on Terror was Bush's idea, and it began in New York and Washington DC on September 11th, 2001. Did you know that it was actually Benjamin Netanyahu's idea, and it began in Israel in the summer of 1979?

Netanyahu is an ultra-radical Zionist and twice-elected Prime Minister of Israel. He launched the War on Terror at the 1979 Jerusalem Conference on International Terrorism (JCIT), which he organized on behalf of the Jonathan Institute, named for his brother who was killed during an IDF raid on the Occupied Territories.[36]

As Nafeez Ahmed writes, the 1979 JCIT "established the ideological foundations for the 'War on Terror.'"[37] Participants at the conference included George H.W. Bush, Richard Pipes, Sen. Henry M. Jackson, Benzion Netanyahu, Shimon Peres, and many other high-level Israeli and U.S. military and intelligence personalities.[38]

Netanyahu's JCIT proposed to deceive the American public, and the world, by wildly exaggerating the dangers of "international terrorism" and even manufacturing a nonexistent "terrorist threat" to mobilize Western populations behind aggressive policies. At exactly the same time as the Jerusalem Conference (summer 1979) Brezezinski and the CIA created al-Qaeda as a CIA asset. The name "al-Qaeda" means "the (data) base" and refers to the CIA's database of Arab fighters that it recruited to battle the Soviets in Afghanistan and elsewhere along the southern flank of the Russian empire. Ahmed cites evidence that "al-Qaeda" does not exist except as a CIA database and a CIA asset. (The Arab/Muslim fighters referred to in the Western press as "al-Qaeda" did not use the term prior to 2001.)

Fast-forward to 1996. Netanyahu, now the Prime Minister of Israel, commissioned a paper entitled "A Clean Break: A New Strategy for Securing the Realm." The paper's lead author was neoconservative Zionist extremist Richard Perle. Co-authors included such neocon Israel-first fanatics as Douglas Feith and David Wurmser—the same folks who would lead the War on Terror propaganda campaign after 9/11.[39] "A Clean Break" argued for (U.S.-imposed) regime change in Iraq. Perle later became the chairman of President George W. Bush's Defense Policy Board, and played a key role in pushing the U.S. into its illegal, fiscally disastrous invasion of Iraq in 2003.[40]

When the Twin Towers were destroyed, and thousands of Americans murdered, Israeli extremists were overjoyed, and the "Clean Break" plan became reality. Netanyahu himself, asked what 9/11 would mean for U.S.-Israeli relations, could barely restrain himself: "It's very good. Well, it's not good, but it will generate immediate sympathy (for Israel)."[41] More than six years later, he hadn't changed his mind:

> The Israeli newspaper Ma'ariv on Wednesday reported that Likud leader Benjamin Netanyahu told an audience at Bar Ilan university that the September 11, 2001 terror attacks had been beneficial for Israel.
>
> "We are benefiting from one thing, and that is the attack on the Twin Towers and Pentagon, and the American struggle in Iraq," Ma'ariv quoted the former prime minister as saying. He reportedly added that these events "swung American public opinion in our favor."[42]

Is the War on Terror a Neoconservative "Noble Lie"?

The neoconservatives are cult followers of Leo Strauss, the University of Chicago philosophy professor who died in 1973. Strauss, a German Jew, was the top student of leading Nazi philosopher Carl Schmitt. Schmitt argued that leaders (like Hitler, and later Bush) are above the law;[43] that all politics is based on scapegoating enemies;[44] that "domestic enemies" (Jews in Germany, Arab/Muslims in America) are legitimate targets;[45] that killing enemies is a very good thing and that moral considerations don't apply, so the mass killing of "enemies" can be engaged in guilt-free.[46] And enemies are so indispensable that if they don't exist, a suitable one must be manufactured.

Strauss was even more extremist than Schmitt.[47] He glorified killing and enmity even more than Schmitt had, then added the doctrine of the "noble lie." Strauss borrowed this idea from Plato, who had argued that a lie that strengthens the nation, and expresses a deeper truth, is a good, noble thing; and from Nietzsche, who claimed that there is no truth, so truth is darkness—the destruction of illusions—rather than light. "Instead of descending into the cave with knowledge of the sunny truth, (Strauss) believes that the role of the philosopher is to manipulate the images in the cave. He teaches that philosophers must fabricate lies for the many while embracing the darkness for themselves. Unwittingly, Strauss cultivates an unprincipled elite whose lies are intended for others and not for themselves."[48]

Strauss was so fanatical in his insistence that the power elite must lie to the people that he turned the story of Socrates upside-down. For Strauss, Socrates is a villain, not a hero. Strauss taught that Socrates deserved to die, because he had committed the one unpardonable crime: he told the truth in public. Strauss actually applauds the murder of Socrates![49] According to leading neocon critic Shadia Drury, Strauss believed the strong should tyrannize the rest: "Those who are fit to rule are those who realize there is no morality and that there is only one natural right, the right of the superior to rule over the inferior."[50]

Neocon Straussians not only advocate the Noble Lie, they support what might be called the Noble Big Lie. The Big Lie was famously described by Hitler:

> They followed the very correct principle, that in the greatness of the lie there is always a certain potency of believability, because the broad masses of people are sooner corrupted in their inmost hearts than they are consciously or intentionally bad; and thus in the primitive simplicity of their nature, they more easily fall victims to the big lie than the

small one, since they themselves sometimes tell little fibs, but would be too ashamed to tell great lies. Such falsehoods do not even occur to them, so they cannot believe others capable of the colossal impudence of these most scandalous distortions. Even when faced with the facts in such a case, they will still linger in doubt and waver and continue to suppose that there must be some truth to it.[51]

For the neocons, the bigger the lie, the more noble. "After all, a great lie, one that is believed, gives form to the void, imposes order on chaos, and creates the world ex nihilo."[52]

Concerning the neocons, Shadia Drury writes that "an elite that identifies its own pursuit of power with the necessary means of preserving Western civilization and preempting catastrophe is bound to be an unprincipled elite, unfit for political power. The loftiness of their enterprise, coupled with their sense of crisis, may lead them to sweep aside moral limits as applicable only to other people."[53]

The Straussian neocon big-liars see themselves as "architects of the lores and legends of society."[54]

Are they the architects of the house (or cage) we now inhabit, the War on Terror—the collection of lores and legends around which our post-9/11 political life revolves?

A key War on Terror architect is Philip Zelikow, the main author of the *9/11 Commission Report*. Zelikow describes himself as a specialist in "the construction and maintenance of public myths" which he describes as "beliefs (1) thought to be true (although not necessarily known to be true with certainty), and (2) shared in common with the relevant political community." Zelikow is especially interested in "'searing' or 'molding' events that take on 'transcendent' importance and, therefore, retain their power even as the experiencing generation passes from the scene."[55] He co-authored a 1998 article in *Foreign Affairs* analyzing the likely political, psychological, and cultural reaction to a massive Pearl Harbor-style terrorist event such as the destruction of the World Trade Center.[56] How did he foresee the near future so accurately? And why was a man with such a background, whose apparent foreknowledge made him a potential suspect, put in charge of the investigation?

Other key neocon War on Terror architects include Paul Wolfowitz, Richard Perle, Dick Cheney, Douglas Feith, Scooter Libby, and Donald Rumsfeld—all members of Project for a New American Century (PNAC), which called for a "New Pearl Harbor" in a document issued in September, 2000. They insisted in that document that the U.S. needed to drastically increase its military budget, launch wars of aggression (euphemistically referred to as "pre-emptive" wars) in the Middle East, remove Saddam Hussein from power in Iraq, and adapt an aggressive new imperial strategy. "The process of transformation is likely to be a long one," they wrote one year before 9/11, "absent some cataclysmic and catalyzing event—like a New Pearl Harbor."[57]

Was 9/11 a "New Pearl Harbor"?

Many scholars believe that President Franklin D. Roosevelt lied about the alleged surprise attack on Pearl Harbor—and that the lie was a justifiable "noble lie." Before Pearl Harbor, American public opinion was overwhelmingly against U.S. entry into the war. Pearl Harbor, some believe, made it possible for the U.S.A. to defeat Hitler. Did Roosevelt manipulate the Japanese with an eight-point plan to force Japan to strike first so as to enrage the American people and allow U.S. entry into the war? Did he know about the attack beforehand and intentionally fail to prevent it? Did he make it happen on purpose by way of the eight-point plan?[58]

Paul Wolfowitz, a student of Strauss and leading neocon geopolitical strategist, has long been fascinated by the immense strategic value of Pearl Harbor, which mobilized America for total war. Wolfowitz has exhibited a lifelong obsession with a remark by Albert Speer to the effect that if Germany had been blessed with a Pearl Harbor it would have won World War II.[59]

If the official myth of the Pearl Harbor surprise attack is a lie, is it a noble lie? Wolfwitz, and the other cult followers of Leo Strauss, would undoubtedly say so.

The popular myth of the dastardly Japanese surprise attack on Pearl Harbor, and the heroic American response, transformed Americans' understanding of themselves and their role in the world. Before Pearl Harbor, Americans agreed that there should be no standing army, and that George Washington's foreign policy of neutrality, non-alignment, and non-involvment in foreign quarrels was the American way.[60] That is why, on the eve of Pearl Harbor, 80% of Americans opposed entering World War II.

After Pearl Harbor, Americans accepted their new role as the world's policeman (some would say the world's biggest bully). A gigantic military-industrial complex mushroomed, and more noble lies were told to gain the people's consent. The negligible military threat to the U.S. posed by the Soviet Union was wildly exaggerated in order to pump up the military budget, and the memory of the alleged sneak attack at Pearl Harbor fed Americans' sense of vulnerability. In this way, an aggressive imperial strategy was made to appear defensive. While pretending to be a purely defensive power, the U.S. regularly threatened other nations with the use of nuclear weapons.[61] It launched illegal, unconstitutional attacks on dozens of nations that posed no threat whatsoever, killing millions of innocent people in the process in what one scholar of U.S. empire, William Blum, has called "the American holocaust."[62]

The Pearl Harbor myth changed history. It turned the U.S.A. from a peace-loving nation into the world's biggest and most aggressive military empire. How did it exert such immense power?

To find out, the U.S. military hired anthropologist Bob Deutch, one of the world's leading experts in using focus groups to understand and manipulate irrational popular beliefs. Deutch discovered that Pearl Harbor shattered Americans' sense of invulnerability: "Because Japan disrupted America's self-mythology of being invincible, the nation would never be forgiven in the irrational American sentiment."[63] Could those who hired Deutch have concluded that a new Pearl Harbor, blamed on Arab Muslims, could provide the kind of "searing or moulding event" that would convince the American public to mobilize for wars on behalf of oil and Israel?

Deutch discovered that at the deep psychological level, the American public, like members of the Hells Angels motorcycle gang, engages in aggression as a defense against a sense of vulnerability and loss: "They are protecting themselves. That's what their core story is about. Images are created to defend loss, not maximize gain."[64]

Another U.S. military psychological expert, S.L.A. Marshall, discovered just how fundamentally defensive and non-aggressive human nature really is, and how powerfully people must be psychologically manipulated if they are to go to war. After an exhaustive study of that vast majority U.S. infantrymen and airmen who, during World War II, covertly refused to kill, Marshall wrote that "the average and healthy individual...has such an inner and usually unrealized resistance towards killing a fellow man that he will not of his own volition take life if it is possible to turn away from that responsibility...At the vital point (the soldier) becomes a conscientious objector."[65] Normal human beings only kill when under direct threat and extreme duress, as a fear-and-anger-inspired defensive response to an aggressor. To motivate a nation to engage in military aggression—mass killing abroad—the people must be brainwashed into believing that they are under attack.

Zbigniew Brezezinski, a leading U.S. foreign policy strategist, notes that the U.S. public's attitude toward the "external projection of American power" is "ambivalent" and depends on the sort of fear and vulnerability awakened by Pearl Harbor: "The public supported America's engagement in World War II largely because of the shock effect of the Japanese attack on Pearl Harbor."[66] Brezezinski's use of the term "shock effect" recalls the thesis of Naomi Klein's *The Shock Doctrine*.[67] According to Klein, individuals and even whole societies can be forced to accept radical, unpleasant changes by way of sudden shocks engineered, or taken advantage of, by unscrupulous elites.

Brezezinski seemed to be calling for a shocking event like 9/11 and the War on Terror it spawned, when he wrote in 1997: "Moreover, as America becomes an increasingly multicultural society, it may find it more difficult to fashion a consensus on foreign policy issues, except in the circumstances of a truly massive and widely perceived direct external threat."[68]

Hollywood, like Brezezinski, seemed to be preparing the American public for 9/11. The run-up to 9/11 saw a rash of patriotic, militaristic, apocalyptic films including the 135 million dollar flop, *Pearl Harbor*.[69] Most American-made action films feature an American hero who is threatened by an evil foreigner, and whose self-defense unfolds into extreme aggression that the audience is taught to accept as legitimate. A grossly disproportionate number of Hollywood's evil foreigners are Arab or Muslim, including in pre-9/11 films.[70] Is this because Hollywood was founded as, and remains, a Jewish enclave with a strong pro-Israeli bias? Or is it because 80% of the world's sweet, easily-extracted oil lies under Arab and Muslim sand, even as an age of energy scarcity looms?[71]

Did 9/11 function as a "new Pearl Harbor" that mobilized Americans for a aggressive war, disguised as a defensive one, against Arab and Muslim countries? T.H. Meyer has called attention to Donald Rumsfeld's bizarre Pearl Harbor propaganda campaign that had begun even before the Bush Administration took office.[72] Rumsfeld spent 2000 and 2001 carrying around extra copies of Roberta *Wohlstetter's Pearl Harbor: Warning and Decision*, praising the book to the skies, and offering free copies to journalists. (Wohlstetter's hawkish Zionist husband Albert, named in his obituary "the world's most influential unknown figure of the past half century," was Wolfowitz's mentor and Richard Perle's father-in-law.)[73] Roberta Wohlstetter's Pearl Harbor book, while it ostensibly supports the official myth that Pearl Harbor was a perfidious surprise attack, includes enough information to the contrary to enlighten the discerning reader to the unspeakable but implicitly acknowledged truth: The Roosevelt Administration provoked the attacks, knew they were coming, and left thousands of sailors in harm's way as an offering to the gods of war. Wohlstetter's book is a perfect illustration of neocon doublespeak: Tell a vivid, simplistic, emotionally-charged lie to the masses ("Perfidious surprise attack! Heroic purple-fury response!") yet include as a subtle subtext the unspeakable truth that only the elite is smart enough to discern and strong enough to handle: *Roosevelt sacrificed thousands of American lives to the greater good of getting the U.S. into the war.*

Rumsfeld's pre-9/11 Pearl Harbor precognitions were echoed on 9/11 itself. On Air Force One, as Bush flew from Florida to Nebraska, the event was already being framed as a new Pearl Harbor.[74] Senator Chuck Hegel and Henry Kissinger quickly echoed the Pearl Harbor comparison. Brezezinski himself pronounced: "It (9/11) is more murderous even than Pearl Harbor, and the psychological impact is the same."[75] On the evening of

September 11th, 2001, George W. Bush reportedly confided to his diary: "The Pearl Harbor of the 21st century took place today."[76]

Before the nano-thermite-laden dust[77] that was all that was left of the World Trade Center had cleared, the corporate media were echoing the Pearl Harbor meme. *Time* Magazine wrote: "What's needed is a unified, unifying, Pearl Harbor sort of purple American fury—a ruthless indignation that doesn't leak away in a week or two."[78] After 9/11 family members shamed a reluctant administration into finally mounting an official investigation, the 9/11 Commission told us that 9/11 was just like Pearl Harbor "except it wasn't the Japanese, but it was al-Qaeda."[79]

But Is "the War on Terror" *Really* Just Like World War II?

Is the War on Terror really like the U.S. war on the axis powers, Japan and Germany? Bush's speechwriter David Frum, a Zionist neocon, tried to suggest as much when he coined the phrase "axis of evil." But do the "axis of evil" nations—Iran, Iraq, and North Korea—have anything to do with each other? Are they an axis at all? And where is the evidence that these nations are evil? Far from constituting a powerful, menacing, aggressive alliance, aren't these nations weak and not part of any alliance?

Are the "Islamofascists" *Really* Just Like the Fascists of the 1930s and 1940s?

The neocon punditocracy, as well as a few neo-neocon pundits like Christopher Hitchens, tried to recall the World War II struggle against fascism by hyping the expression *islamofascism*. The term *fascism* means the militarization of society under the jackboot of a government that has merged with corporate power (which is why fascism's other name is "corporatism.") But do not most political scientists agree that world's Islamic nations are not fascist, because they are neither heavily militarized nor merged with corporate power? Isn't it the case that Islamic culture tends to rebuff corporate power, especially that of the usurious international financiers who are the real force behind the U.S. military's international power grab?[80] Is not military weakness, not strength, the real reason the Islamic world has been plagued by wars? Islamic countries including Palestine, Chechnya, Algeria, Iraq, Bosnia, Kashmir,

36

Afghanistan, and the Central Asian republics formerly colonized by Russia have all been victimized by wars of aggression during the past century. Were they not victimized because they, along with other Muslim countries, were militarily weak? Might it not be desirable, in the interest of world peace, that Muslim nations be strengthened militarily to the point they can deter potential aggressors? Is this not an entirely different geopolitical situation than the world faced when Hitler's armies overran Europe? (And a very different situation than the one portrayed in today's mainstream media, where one nuclear weapon in Iran is considered intolerable, while hundreds in Israel are unremarkable?)

Will It Ever End?

The U.S. entered World War II in December, 1941. The war ended victoriously on August 14th, 1945. It lasted a little over three-and-a-half years.

The War on Terror was declared on or about September 11th, 2001. It still continues eight years later, with no victory in sight. If anything, the U.S. seems to be losing. The Iraqi people are almost unanimously hostile and want the U.S. to leave; the only thing the Sunnis and Shiites can agree on is that the U.S. should pack its bags ASAP and go home. Even the quisling U.S. puppet government in Iraq has been forced by public opinion to demand quick U.S. withdrawal.[81] Meanwhile the people of Afghanistan are increasingly rising up in fury to resist the criminal occupation of their country.[82] And the U.S. economy, sapped by this multi-trillion-dollar "war," continues its downward spiral.

How could this war possibly end victoriously, as World War II did? Indeed, how could it end at all? How can "terror" be defeated?

Was the War on Terror *designed* to be endless? When Cheney speaks of "the war that will not end in our lifetimes," and McCain talks of a "100 years war," are they telling us that the war cannot end, and that this is precisely the point? Are they taking a page from Orwell's *1984*, which posits an endless war against a mythical, demonized enemy? If so, is their purpose the same as that of Orwell's Party: to use lies and fear to control the population?

Which Country or Countries Are We Fighting, and Why?

When the War on Terror began, the four declared enemies were Afghanistan, Iraq, Iran, and North Korea. Pakistan was our close ally.

Today, the allegedly evil and oppressive governments in Afghanistan and Iraq have been deposed, yet we're still there, fighting the Afghani and Iraqi people—the victims of the regimes we deposed. North Korea has been forgotten, even though it has flaunted Bush's orders and developed and deployed nuclear weapons (unlike the other three countries). And in a bizarre and seemingly pointless shift, we may be launching a war of aggression against Pakistan, and opening dipolomatic relations with Iran, a country we were on the brink of invading just a few moments ago.

What does any of this have to do with "terror"? What is this endless war against an endlessly-shifting array of enemies supposed to accomplish? Isn't it reminiscent of *1984* and the Party's war against Eastasia, which suddenly became a war against Eurasia for no reason at all?

Is There a Pharmaceutical Solution?

If we are really trying to conquer "terror," defined as "extreme fear," might there be a pharmaceutical solution? There are plenty of anti-anxiety medications out there. Could we "win" the war by dosing our own water supply with tranquilizers? Or is television, the main source of anxiety, also the tranquilizer? Does TV operate as a social control tool, first by fostering fear, then by tranquilizing the population with platitudes? Would switching from television to tranquilizers solve the problem? Is the TV-B-Gone, a remote-control television-killing device, the ultimate weapon against terror?[83]

Is the War on Terror an Excuse for War Crimes?

The War on Terror unleashed a horrendous chain of war crimes. Tens of thousands of innocent people have been arbitrarily arrested, detained, and in many cases brutally tortured or even murdered. In Afghanistan, roughly 4,500 Afghani men were packed into in cargo containers and slowly broiled to death in the hot sun, without access to water, under the supervision of U.S. special forces and

38

CIA officers.[84] These men died an unimaginably horrible death as they clawed each other in hopes of obtaining a drop of blood. Before opening the cargo containers to clean out the corpses, thugs under observation by U.S. special forces and CIA officers riddled the containers with bullets.[85]

Compared to this, the Nazis' treatment of Jews was positively humane. After all, nobody was slowly broiled to death in the cattle cars en route to Auschwitz.

Unfortunately, the "convoy of death" massacre was not an isolated incident. Under the Bush regime, nearly 80,000 Muslim men were kidnapped by U.S. government agents and held in horrendous conditions in illegal Abu Ghraib style torture camps all over the world.[86] These concentration camps blatantly flaunt the Geneva Convention, UN minimum standards for the treatment of prisoners, and the Universal Declaration of Human Rights. Torture and murder are routine, and perpetrators are rarely if ever punished. Moazzam Begg, for example, witnessed a fellow prisoner being murdered by guards, and experienced horrendous treatment despite being cooperative and fluent in English. Begg, a completely innocent man, was even tortured into signing a ridiculous false confession.[87] Based on reports by Begg and others, it is clear that torture is being practiced routinely throughout the worldwide gulag of concentration camps, and that the vast majority of kidnapping victims (or "detainees" as they are euphemistically called) are innocent civilians who have been caught up in sweeps or turned in for bounties. While a minority of these prisoners are soldiers who fought with the pre-2002 Afghan government to defend Afghanistan against an illegal invasion from abroad, that is hardly a crime that merits sub-P.O.W. treatment, much less torture.

The well-known cases of torture and sexual abuse at Abu Ghraib are, unfortunately, only the tip of the iceberg. Seymour Hersh reports that U.S. guards in Iraq filmed themselves sodomizing Iraqi children in front of their parents, as a psychological torture technique directed at the parents. Hersh, who has seen the videos, told an ACLU Crossroads conference that "The worst is the soundtrack of the boys shrieking." Here is a transcript of Hersh's talk:

Some of the worse that happened that you don't know about, ok. Videos, there are women there. Some of you may have read they were passing letters, communications out to their men. This is at Abu Ghraib which is 30 miles from Baghdad [...]

The women were passing messages saying "Please come and kill me, because of what's happened." Basically what happened is that those women who were arrested with young boys/children in cases that have been recorded. The boys were sodomized with the cameras rolling. The worst about all of them is the soundtrack of the boys shrieking that your government has. They are in total terror it's going to come out.

It's impossible to say to yourself how do we get there? who are we? Who are these people that sent us there?[88]

Remember, you're more likely to drown in your bathtub or get hit by lightning than to die from terrorism. So how did the War on Terror become an excuse for sodomizing children?

Why So Much Torture?

Recent revelations suggest that since 9/11, the U.S. government has been torturing people on a massive and unprecedented scale. Granted, U.S. government torture predates the Cheney-Bush administration. The CIA has a long history of researching and practicing torture techniques.[89] But before Bush, torture was the exception rather than the rule. And, of course, it was officially illegal.

Post-9/11, all that changed. As we have seen, many, perhaps most, of the 80,000 innocent Muslims (along with an alleged handful of guilty ones) who have gone through Guantanamo, Bagram, and the dozens of other outposts of the global terror gulag have been tortured. How did the U.S. change so rapidly from defender of human rights to world's leading torturing nation?

Immediately after 9/11, such apologists for torture as radical Zionist law professor Alan Dershowitz launched a pro-torture PR offensive. In a series of speeches, op-eds and TV appearances, Dershowitz urged that torture be legalized and normalized. Why?

Because "society needs to be protected from immigrants and other undesirables."[90]

In this as in all other matters, Dershowitz takes his cues from the state of Israel, the only nation on earth that has legalized torture. Dershowitz and other members of the post-9/11 pro-torture propaganda operation—most of whom are also radical Zionists—endlessly rehash the "ticking time bomb" scenario cited by the Israeli Supreme Court in its 1987 legalization of torture: *What if terrorists were about to explode a nuclear weapon in an Israeli (or American) city, and we caught one of them? Couldn't we torture him to reveal the location of the ticking nuclear time bomb?*

While plausible at first glance, this argument falls apart under scrutiny. First, the scenario is wildly unlikely. Whatever the chances of nuclear terrorists bombing a city, the odds that the first time this was about to happen, one of the terrorists with specific where-and-when knowledge would be captured just in the nick of time...well, let's just say that this is about as likely as being attacked by flying radioactive Elvises from outer space. In other words, we may expect thousands of terrorists to succeed in blowing up thousands of our cities long before we happen to catch one just at the right moment to deploy the ticking-time-bomb torture scenario. Secondly, accepting for the sake of argument that such a wildly improbable scenario could actually happen, any terrorist with even a minimal commitment to his cause would obviously give one or more false locations for the ticking time bomb, buying plenty of time for the bomb to go off. Torturers and other experts know that torture is useless for extracting timely and accurate information. The torture victim is motivated to say something, anything, to stop the torture. A committed terrorist will give false information if this will help his cause. Only after a long period of torture will a torture victim "break" and tell the truth—though by this time his mind may be so far gone that he won't even know what the truth is. Once broken, the torture victim becomes a virtual blank slate for the interrogator to control.[91]

According to a 2009 McClatchey Newspapers story, Dick Cheney lied outrageously when he claimed that the torture programs he instituted "prevented the violent death of thousands, if not hundreds of thousands, of innocent people."[92] Cheney cited

Admiral Dennis Blair, Director of National Intelligence, for his claim that torture saved lives. But what Blair actually said was that "there is no way of knowing whether the same information could have been obtained through other means. The bottom line is that these techniques hurt our image around the world, the damage they have done to our interests far outweighed whatever benefit they gave us and they are not essential to our national security."

If, as the experts say, torture does not yield timely and accurate information, then why has the U.S. government been torturing so many people?

U.S. Senator Carl Levin offers the most plausible answer: "The (CIA's torture) techniques are based on tactics used by Chinese Communists against American soldiers during the Korean War *for the purpose of eliciting false confessions for propaganda purposes* (emphasis mine)...the person will say whatever he believes will stop the pain."[93] According to a Senate report on detainee abuse, "Rumsfeld, former Secretary of State Condoleezza Rice, and other former senior Bush administration officials were responsible for the abusive interrogation techniques used at Guantanamo and in Iraq and Afghanistan" and that the torture policy's original purpose was to produce false confessions linking Iraq to 9/11.[94]

And speaking of false confessions, the London *Times* points out: "Khalid Sheikh Mohammed, the self-confessed mastermind of 9/11, was waterboarded 183 times in one month, and 'confessed' to murdering the journalist Daniel Pearl, which he did not. There could hardly be more compelling evidence that such techniques are neither swift, nor efficient, nor reliable."[95] The kind of intensive long term torture inflicted on KSM is normally intended not for extracting timely information, but for destroying the victim's personality, including his or her accurate and truthful memories, so that a new, programmable personality can be constructed.[96]

The 9/11 Commission's account of the 19-Muslims-with-box-cutters plot relied almost entirely on secondhand accounts of confessions allegedly extracted from KSM under torture. The only evidence that KSM had anything to do with 9/11, other than KSM's own statements under torture, came from another torture victim, Abu Zubaida. But according to Daniel Coleman, the FBI's point man on the Abu Zubaida investigation that led to the identification of KSM as a 9/11 suspect, Abu Zubaida was a schizophrenic who would never have been trusted with any serious information.[97] Was the schizophrenic Zubaida's statement (under torture) that KSM was involved in 9/11 reliable? Was KSM tortured into producing a false confession to support a pre-scripted official account of 9/11? If not, why has the CIA illegally destroyed the evidence surrounding the interrogations of KSM, Abu Zubaida, and other "high-value detainees"?[98] Were these detainees "high-value" not because they had anything to do with 9/11, but because they were tortured into rubber-stamping a pre-scripted official account, making them high-value propaganda patsies? The CIA's former top on-the-ground agent in the Middle East, Robert Baer, was stunned by revelations that CIA torturers destroyed the key evidence behind the government's version of 9/11: "I would find it very difficult to believe the CIA would deliberately destroy evidence material to the 9/11 investigation, evidence that would cover up a core truth, such as who really was behind 9/11. On the other hand I have to wonder what space-time continuum the CIA exists in, if they weren't able to grasp what a field day the 9/11 conspiracy theorists are going to have with this..."[99] (Baer himself, who now says "the evidence points to" 9/11 being an inside job, has apparently joined the conspiracy theorists who are now having a field day.)[100]

Are the Terror Wars Illegal?

Torture, rape, sodomizing children...as awful as such war crimes are, critics argue that they are dwarfed by the supreme war crime: the illegal invasion and occupation of two sovereign nations, Afghanistan and Iraq. According to international law, any attack on another country, in the absence of a grave and immanent threat, is a crime. The name of that crime is "aggression."

To get an idea of just HOW illegal these invasions and occupations are, remember that the Nazis were tried, convicted, and sentenced to death for the supreme war crime: aggression. As post-World War II International Military Tribunal at Nuremberg put it, the waging of aggressive war "essentially an evil thing...to initiate a war of aggression...is not only an international crime; it is the supreme international crime, differing only from other war crimes in that it contains within itself the accumulated evil of the whole."[101]

According to international law and basic morality, aggression is worse than raping children, worse than torturing people to death in boxcars, worse even than genocide. Why? Because starting a war, by invading someone else's country, leads to all the other crimes and disasters, including genocide. Hitler's illegal invasion of Poland led to the deaths of more than 60 million people, while the Holocaust killed fewer than one-tenth that many. That is why the Nazis were hanged at Nuremburg for aggression—the supreme war crime, the worst crime a human being can commit. (Bush's wars have killed more than a million people so far, according to *The Lancet*, one of the world's leading medical journals.)[102]

Since World War II, the world's community of nations have agreed that aggression is the supreme war crime. No third world war has broken out, because large-scale naked aggression has been taboo (and, of course, supremely illegal). When the Russians invaded Czechoslovakia and Afghanistan, as when the U.S.A. invaded Korea and Vietnam, a pretense of having been "invited" by the "legitimate government" of the target country was always proffered. Was this pretense hypocritical? Of course. But as LaRochefoucault's epigram puts it, "Hypocrisy is the tribute vice pays to virtue." By the universal agreement among nations to pay tribute to the virtue of non-aggression, the world has avoided the Last World War—the war that, if it happens, will kill us all. That universal agreement lasted from 1946 until 2001. Then Bush and Cheney invaded Afghanistan and Iraq. Now, all bets are off. The Last World War could break out at any time. For all we know, it has already begun.

Were the invasions of Afghanistan and Iraq the worst war crimes since the Nazis invaded Poland—perhaps even the worst war crimes ever, the war crimes that will destroy humanity? I leave that for you, and history, to judge.

Is the War on Terror Really a War on Islam and Muslims?

Many of the world's 1.5 billion Muslims think so. Nearly half believe the War on Terror's primary goal is to weaken and divide the Islamic world, while almost three-quarters agree that the U.S. is trying to do this. [103]

James Schall, Professor of Government at Georgetown University, agrees. "I always thought it was a mistake not to say what Iraq really was, that is, a war against an expanding Islam," says Schall, who writes papers for the Hoover Institute, a key neocon think tank.[104]

If, as Schall suggests, the War on Terror is really a war on Islam, Bernard Lewis deserves much of the credit for launching it. Lewis, a staunchly pro-Zionist Jew of British origin, coined the term "clash of civilizations" (later popularized by Samuel Huntington) in his 1990 essay "The Roots of Muslim Rage."[105] Edward Said notes that Lewis's view of history "is a crudely Darwinian one in which powers and cultures vow for dominance, some rising, some sinking."[106]

Lewis seems obsessed with the specter of Islam rising. His bestseller *What Went Wrong*, written before 9/11 and published in the wake of the attacks, postulates that there is something wrong with Islam, and sets out to explain just what it is and how it got there. In fact, Lewis claims to find many things wrong with Islam and Muslims, including sexism, self-absorption, failure to appreciate Western classical music, and a desire for wealth and power. Lewis claims, above all, that power-obsessed Muslims obsessively ask what went wrong with their civilization that allowed the West to overtake them—and then ask themselves how to overcome that disadvantage and defeat the West. Thus the title *What Went Wrong* also hints at another meaning: It is the question Westerners will have to ask themselves if they are stupid enough to let the Muslims overtake the West once again. To forestall that horrid possibility, Lewis advocates bellicosity against Muslim allies and enemies alike.

Samuel Huntington took up Lewis's idea and ran with it. In his immensely influential 1993 essay "The Clash of Civilizations," Huntington famously argued that future wars would not be fought for economic or ideological reasons.[107] Instead, they would be fought between different civilizations. And the most likely clash, he argued, was between Islam and the West. "Islam has bloody borders," Huntington wrote, ignoring the fact that in virtually all cases it is Muslims who have been attacked, invaded and occupied along those borders by non-Muslim aggressors.[108] Like Lewis,

Huntington drops hints that he fears for the future of Western civilization in the face of the rise of Islam. His Spenglerian gloom and doom surfaces in such passages as: "Civilizations are dynamic; they rise and fall; they divide and merge. And, as any student of history knows, civilizations disappear and are buried in the sands of time."[109]

After the 9/11-anthrax attacks, Huntington was hailed as a prophet. But could his have been a self-serving and self-fulfilling prophecy? As a Cold War defense intellectual, Huntington spent most of his life justifying inflated U.S. military budgets by overstating the Soviet threat. In 1990, the Soviet Union disappeared, taking with it the justification for massive U.S. military spending. A few years later, "The Clash of Civilizations" replaced the Cold War as the ideological basis of astronomical military budgets.

In *The War on Islam*, Enver Masud writes:

> The fear of Islamic fundamentalism, militancy, radicalism, terrorism, totalitarianism, and the West's discovery of the "rogue states," appeared quite conveniently with the fall of the Berlin Wall, and the disintegration of the Soviet Union. Former Defense Secretary McNamara, in his 1989 testimony before the Senate Budget Committee, said U.S. defense spending could safely be cut in half. It became clear that the U.S. either had to undergo massive shifts in spending, a painful and unwelcome prospect for the defense establishment, or find new justification for continuing high levels of military expenditures.

That new justification, of course, was "militant Islam." In Masud's view, the "civilizational enemy" talk conceals the fact that Islam is an enemy of convenience. For Masud, the "war on Islam" justifies military budgets and wars whose purpose is more geostrategic than religious.

If Islam poses a geopolitical threat to the West, it certainly isn't a military one. No Muslim-majority country has invaded and occupied any Western country—or any non-Muslim-majority country for that matter—in centuries! The West, however, has invaded and occupied much of the Muslim world. While we like to think that the imperial-colonial era is over, the fact is that it continues today. European Jewish invaders continue to occupy

Palestine, the second-holiest Islamic land. Spain continues to occupy Moroccan coastal cities. The US continues to occupy Afghanistan and Iraq. While Muslims have had occasional success repelling Western occupations, there is little or no prospect that Muslims will have the desire or capability to attack and conquer Western nations in the foreseeable future.

While Islamic nations and Islamic civilization offer no realistic military threat to the West, some argue that they pose a long-term economic and demographic threat. If the price of oil continues to skyrocket, say the alarmists, the Islamic nations (which have 80% of earth's remaining high-quality oil) will grow wealthier and more powerful, eventually tipping the balance of power in their favor.

Even worse than the economic threat, in the alarmist view, is the Islamic demographic threat. Pat Buchanan sums it up:

> In Europe, Christian congregations are dying, churches are emptying out, and mosques are filling up. There are five million Muslims in France, and between twelve and fifteen million in the European Union. There are fifteen hundred mosques in Germany. Islam has replaced Judaism as the second religion of Europe. As the Christian tide goes out in Europe, and Islamic tide comes in. In 2000, for the first time there were more Muslims in the world than Catholics.[110]

But few sober analysts expect an Islamic world takeover. Demographers point out that Muslim birthrates are falling faster than those in any other culture. According to RAND Corporation political scientist Brian Nichiporuk, "there is a demographic transition going on in the Muslim world. We are starting to see across-the-board decreases in fertility rates, even in the high fertility countries."[111] Spengler of the *Asia Times* opines that "the Muslim world half a century from now can expect the short end of the stick from the modern world. It has generated only two great surpluses, namely people and oil. By the middle of the century both of these will have begun to dwindle."[112]

Whatever the motivations of the "War on Terror," it cannot have been born out of any realistic fear that Muslims are likely to take over the world, or that Islamic nations or Islamic extremists pose a meaningful military threat to the U.S.

Do They Really Hate Our Freedom?

Ever since 9/11, the authorities have repeated the mantra "they hate our freedom." But what does that mean, if anything? Assuming it means something, is it true?

History professor Patrick Rael argues that "of all the misinformation, half-truths, and outright lies about terrorism put forth by the Bush Administration, none is as pernicious" as the myth that *they hate our freedom.*[113] According to Dr. Rael, even Bin Laden himself does not hate freedom.

Bin Laden may or may not have had something to do with 9/11. Though the US media has fostered the impression of his guilt, Bin Laden is on record repeatedly and categorically denying any involvement and deploring the 9/11 attacks as un-Islamic, first saying "I would like to assure the world that I did not plan the recent attacks, which seems to have been planned by people for personal reasons,"[114] and later "I had no knowledge of these attacks, nor do I consider the killing of innocent women, children and other humans as an appreciable act."[115] The FBI apparently agrees, stating that Bin Laden is "not wanted" for 9/11 because there is "no hard evidence" against him.[116] But at least until his reported death in December, 2001,[117] Bin Laden did lash out at the USA with harsh words, and he did at least encourage (and possibly help organize) military attacks on US forces and interests.[118] Though the FBI doesn't blame him for 9/11, they do assert his criminal liability for the African embassy bombings and the attack on the U.S.S. Cole.[119]

So why did Bin Laden support, and possibly help organize, attacks on U.S. embassies and military vessels? Because he "hated our freedom"? According to history professor Patrick Rael:

> To the contrary, bin Laden believes he is acting on behalf of freedom. Were we actually to listen to bin Laden, we would hear him employing the same rhetoric of liberty as does Bush. "We fight because we are free men who don't sleep under oppression," bin Laden has said. "We want to restore freedom to our nation, just as you lay waste to our nation." Last December, bin Laden said that Bush was wrong to

claim that al-Qaeda hated freedom. "If so, then let him explain to us why we don't strike, for example, Sweden."[120]

So if Bin Laden loved freedom, why has he used verbal and perhaps physical violence against the U.S.? Rael points out that Bin Laden "has consistently pointed to three factors in justifying his actions: the presence of U.S. troops on Saudi soil, U.N. sanctions against Iraq, and Israel's policy toward its Arab neighbors."[121] From the Arab and Muslim perspectives, all of those are pro-freedom, not anti-freedom, positions.

The idea that Islamists in general "hate freedom" is promoted by propagandists who equate freedom with the right to appear in public barely dressed and the right to choose between rum & Coke and bourbon & Pepsi. In reality Islamist parties in much of the Muslim world are fighting for freedom and democracy against brutal, repressive dictatorships propped up by the USA on behalf of Israel and oil. Islamists want the freedom to speak out without being arrested and tortured; to organize Islamic charitable and social institutions; to reduce corruption in government; to choose non-usurious financial systems; to repeal laws prohibiting headscarfs in public places so women can control their own appearance; to say "no" to the international bankers who are bent on taking over their countries and exploiting their resources; to decide which dangerous drugs (such as alcohol) are licit and which are illicit based on their own culture rather than someone else's; the right to use their own legal system rather than someone else's; and so on. No wonder the Islamists say they are working *for* freedom, not against it.

Most Islamist as well as non-Islamist Muslims love American freedom, at least most aspects of it. Muslims have immigrated to the USA by the millions to partake of freedom of opportunity and freedom of speech. They love our freedom, and they hate to see it taken away—as it has been since 9/11.

Is "Terrorism" the Real Reason We Invaded Afghanistan?

The War on Terror doubled the U.S. military budget and triggered invasions of Afghanistan and Iraq. But what did those wars have to do with "terrorism"?

Did we really invade Afghanistan because Osama Bin Laden was there? Most Americans still think so. But there are problems with this conspiracy theory.

"Conspiracy" means two or more people working together to commit a crime or immoral action. "Theory" means an attempt to explain a group of facts. Those who think Bush invaded Afghanistan in pursuit of Osama believe in three conspiracies. First, they think Osama conspired with 19 young Arabs to pull off 9/11. Second, they think members of the Taliban government conspired to prevent Osama from being brought to justice. Third, they think Bush Administration members and others conspired to commit an illegal invasion of Afghanistan because they wanted to get Osama.

All three of these conspiracy theories are questionable.

We will leave off questioning 9/11 itself until the end of the book. For now, suffice it to say that the FBI asserts that Osama Bin Laden is "not wanted" for 9/11 because there is "no hard evidence" against him.[122] Indeed, Bin Laden has never been indicted for 9/11.[123] So the "Osama and 19 young Arabs" conspiracy theory may be popular in the media, but it is questioned by no less an authority than the FBI.

What about the theory that the Taliban conspired to prevent Bin Laden from being brought to justice? It's a great theory. However, the facts indicate otherwise. The Taliban offered to hand over Bin Laden for trial prior to and during the initial U.S. bombing of Afghanistan in October, 2001.[124] In fact, they repeatedly offered to hand him over at least 20 times *before* 9/11, according to the *Washington Post*.[125] The problem was, the Taliban wanted to follow international law. So they asked to see some sort of evidence—any evidence—of Bin Laden's guilt. Bush refused, saying "There's no need to discuss innocence or guilt. We know he's guilty."[126] That's funny...Bush "knew" Bin Laden was guilty of 9/11 in October, 2001? How did he know that? As we just saw, today the FBI insists that Bin Laden is "not wanted" for 9/11 because there is "no hard evidence" against him.[127] How can we explain the contradiction? Does the conspiracy theory that the Taliban conspired to prevent Bin Laden from being brought to justice hold water? Or is it the

Bush Administration, rather than the Taliban, that was obstructing justice?

And how about the theory that the Bush Administration, along with the military and CIA, conspired to invade Afghanistan in pursuit of Bin Laden? If their purpose was to snatch a fugitive, would a massive military invasion, preceded by open warnings, really make sense? If they didn't have enough evidence to convince the Taliban to hand him over, but still wanted to snatch him, wouldn't they send small teams of undercover covert operators to launch a surprise raid, without any warning? And wouldn't that be a lot cheaper than a massive, permanent military occupation of the whole country?

And if the Bush Administration really wanted to catch Bin Laden and his associates, why did it seemingly go out of its way to let them escape? After American forces and their Northern Alliance had surrounded Kabul November 2001, a huge convoy of "at least 1,000 cars and trucks" carrying top al-Qaeda leaders, presumably including Bin Laden, jammed the main road out of Kabul from eight a.m. until three a.m.; a local businessman said "it must have been easy for American planes to see the headlights."[128] People in Kabul knew what was going on and were amazed that the Americans, who had Kabul under a microscope, didn't bomb the convoy. "We don't understand how they weren't all killed" said one local businessman.[129]

From Kabul, al-Qaeda forces moved to Jalalabad, and U.S. intelligence agencies reported that Bin Laden was among them. A Knight-Ridder news report described how, once again, U.S. forces seemed to go out of their way to let Bin Laden escape:

> American intelligence analysts concluded that bin Laden and his retreating fighters were preparing to flee across the border. But the U.S. Central Command, which was running the war, made no move to block their escape. "It was obvious from at least early November that this area was to be the base for an exodus into Pakistan," said one intelligence official, who spoke only on condition of anonymity. "All of this was known, and frankly we were amazed that nothing was done to prepare for it."[130]

On November 14th, the U.S.-directed Northern Alliance took Jalalabad. That night, once again, a huge al-Qaeda convoy of over 1,000 vehicles openly left town without any interference. As the massive convoy pulled out, U.S. planes bombed the Jalalabad Airport but allowed Bin Laden and his thousands of associates to escape by land.[131]

From Jalalabad, Bin Laden and his followers reached Tora Bora. American planes bombed one of the two roads from Tora Bora to Pakistan, but left the other one alone. Naturally, Bin Laden and friends took the road that was free from interference. U.S. troops could have easily been assigned to blockade all escape routes. Instead, the U.S. military surrounded the al-Qaeda convoy on three sides only, leaving an open road to Pakistan. According to the London *Telegraph*, "the battle for Tora Bora looks more like a grand charade."[132] Tora Bora locals and American whistleblowers say that mysterious black helicopters came and went unimpeded by U.S. forces, ferrying al-Qaeda and Taliban leaders to safety in Pakistan.[133]

Not long after U.S. forces apparently went out of their way to let Bin Laden escape—and just six months after the destruction of the World Trade Center—Bush said of Bin Laden: "I truly am not that concerned about him."[134] Gen. Richard Meyers, the acting head of the Joint Chiefs of Staff on 9/11, seconded Bush's remarks, saying "The goal has never been to get Bin Laden."[135] An anonymous U.S. official explained: "'Casting our objectives too narrowly' risked 'a premature collapse of the international effort if by some lucky chance Mr. bin Laden was captured.'"[136] Not all U.S. officials agreed with the let-'em-go strategy. One said, "It's not a f_ckup, it's an outrage."[137]

In short, the evidence is overwhelming: The conspiracy theory that Bush invaded Afghanistan to get bin Laden is false. Then why *did* the Bush Administration and its Pentagon and CIA conspire to commit an illegal invasion of Afghanistan?

Afghanistan is important economically for two reasons. First, it is a site for oil and gas pipeline routes from the Caspian Sea basin. Second, it is the world's leading producer of opium, the raw material for heroin.

As all police investigators know, when a crime is committed, the first question is "who benefits?"and the prime imperative is "follow the money." Let's explore possible economic motives for the Bush Administration's illegal invasion of Afghanistan.

Was the Invasion of Afghanistan Really About Oil and Gas?[138]

Many experts think so. According to Karl Schwartz, the conservative Republican CEO of Patmos Nanotechnologies and an energy business insider:

> Some time around 2000, there was an "investment club" created. It was somewhere around $20 to $22 billion dollars and was promoted by a lot of high profile names mentioned often in this 9-11 / Caspian Basin fiasco, and some not mentioned at all. Names like George H W Bush, Tricky Dick Cheney, Nicholas Brady, John Sununu and others. All of their names surfaced in our investigation of what was going on in the Caspian Basin. They had all purchased front row seats to get at those trillions, and trillions and trillions of dollars in Caspian oil and gas.[139]

In their bestseller *Bin Laden: The Forbidden Truth*, Jean-Charles Brisard and Guillaume Dasquie present evidence that prior to July, 2001 the Bush Administration was trying to cut a deal with the Taliban. Bush's goal: Help Unocal get a contract to build an Afghan pipeline offering access to the vast Caspian Basin gas and oil reserves. But the Taliban was holding out for a better deal. When the Taliban blew off Bush and Unocal, and gave the pipeline contract to the Argentine company Bridas, U.S. officials summoned Taliban leaders to the famous July, 2001 Berlin conference where U.S. official Tom Simons delivered an ultimatim: "Either you accept our offer of a carpet of gold, or we bury you under a carpet of bombs."[140] Former Pakistani Foreign Secretary Niaz Naik says he was told by senior American officials at the July, 2001 Berlin Conference that the U.S. invasion of Afghanistan was planned to "take place before the snows started falling in Afghanistan, by the middle of October at the latest."[141]

The timeline raises obvious questions: How could the US invasion of Afghanistan have been set in motion two months before

9/11, despite the fact that it would have been politically impossible had 9/11 not occurred? Did they know 9/11 was coming?

As we have seen, the U.S. invaders did not go after Bin Laden. Instead, they built a string of military bases. According to the Israeli newspaper Ma'ariv, "If one looks at the map of the big American bases (in Afghanistan) one is struck by the fact that they are completely identical to the route of the projected oil pipeline to the Indian Ocean."[142]

Bush appointed Hamid Karzai, a former Unocal executive, as president of occupied Afghanistan. He also named another Unocal figure, Zalmay Khalilzad, as his special envoy to Afghanistan. Plans for the trans-Afghanistan pipeline continued after the U.S. invasion, but have been delayed due to the insurgency. Meanwhile, while the U.S. has been alienating the whole world, especially the Muslim world, with its war crimes, Russia has quietly seized control of the Caspian Sea energy bonanza. In July 2008, Russia cut a historic deal with Turkmenistan formalizing Russian control over all Turkmen gas exports. An *Asia Times* article put bluntly: "In the geopolitics of energy security, nothing like this has happened before. The United States has suffered a huge defeat in the race for Caspian gas."[143] Karl Schwartz put it even more bluntly:

> The game is over. It is checkmate.
>
> As I have predicted all along, George W Bush lost his Global War on Terror because it was all based on lies from the outset.
>
> The U.S. and UK lost the GWOT to take over the Caspian Basin and Iran. The Grand Chessboard scheme is a total failure and we lost. [144]

Was It Also About Heroin?

Along with energy, the other economically significant product of Afghanistan is opium, the raw material for heroin. Afghanistan's opium crop produces 90% of the world's heroin.[145] The global illegal drug trade, worth more than 500 billion dollars per year, serves as the prime engine of the world's 1.5 trillion dollar per year money laundering industry. The global money laundering industry is bigger than all but the world's five biggest economies.[146]

During the year prior to the U.S. invasion, the Taliban shut down Afghanistan's opium production—by far the biggest and most successful anti-drug move by any nation in modern history. When the Taliban eradicated the Afghan opium crop, thereby virtually destroying the global heroin industry, former LAPD narcotics detective Mike Ruppert called it "an act of economic warfare that might take a whole lot of money out of the world's banking system and its cooked books."[147] Ruppert explains most of the annual 1.5 trillion dollar harvest of dirty money is laundered through the world's biggest banks and corporations, meaning that drug money is an essential pillar of the global financial system.

Was the U.S. invasion of Afghanistan partly a response to the Taliban's act of economic warfare? Bush's invasion of Afghanistan happened in November 2001, in the middle of the opium planting season. Ruppert writes: "Among the first things the U.S. forces and CIA did was to liberate a number of known opium warlords... Opium farmers rejoiced and, amidst reports that they were being encouraged to do so, began planting massive opium crops."[148]

By 2003 the Afghan opium crop had bounced back to record levels. Since then, production has skyrocketed, as reflected by a series of record-breaking years. The *Washington Post* wrote that official attempts to blame the heroin boom on Taliban insurgents are misleading, saying the real reasons include "corruption and alliances formed by Washington and the Afghan government with anti-Taliban tribal chieftains, some of whom are believed to be deeply involved in the trade."[149] The *Post* noted that by 2006 Afghan opium production was nearly double its highest pre-Hamid Karzai level.

Could the Afghanistan invasion have been intended, at least in part, to restore stability and profits to big banks threatened by the Taliban's annihilation of the global heroin industry? It sounds outlandish. But when the facts themselves are outlandish, sometimes only outlandish-sounding theories can explain them.

Was "Terrorism" the Real Reason the Bush Administration Invaded Iraq?

We have examined the various conspiracy theories, including the official conspiracy theory, that attempt to explain why the Bush

Administration illegally invaded Afghanistan. So now let's look at some Iraq war conspiracy theories, including the official one.

As we have seen, the invasion of Iraq was clearly illegal—a clear-cut case of the supreme war crime, aggression. Since more than one person was involved in planning and executing this crime, there is no question about it being a conspiracy. Nor is there much question about who the conspirators were. The question is, why did they do it? What was the real motive?

The criminals themselves tell us that their motive was "fighting terror." They claim they invaded Iraq as part of the "War on Terror." They claimed that Saddam Hussein's government had weapons of mass destruction, and that Hussein was likely to use these WMDs in terrorist attacks on the U.S.A. The only way to stop this apocalyptic threat, they said, was a U.S. invasion of Iraq.

In 2003, the American people were still scared out of their wits by the sensationalist media coverage of 9/11 and the follow-up anthrax attack (which, as we have seen, together killed about the number of people who die from cigarettes every few days). Wildly exaggerated fears of terrorism led most Americans to overlook the illegality of Bush's proposed war of aggression against Iraq.

But did Hussein really have WMD, and if he did, would he have even contemplated using it in terrorist attacks in the U.S.A.? The answer to both questions is "no."

The U.S. invasion itself was proof that Hussein had no operational WMD capability, and that Bush knew it. If Hussein had possessed WMD, he surely would have used it against invading U.S. forces. There could have been no U.S. invasion had there even been a slight chance that Hussein had operational WMD.

If Hussein, or any other leader of a relatively small country that opposes U.S. policies, *did* get hold of operational WMD, would they use it to launch terrorist attacks in the U.S.A.? Not likely. If Iraq or North Korea (or Russia or China for that matter) launched WMD terror attacks in the U.S.A., they would be guaranteeing the total incineration of their own countries. The only use of WMD is to deter attack. Some would even say that it's too bad for America that Hussein *didn't* have a strong WMD capability, because if he had, it would have prevented Bush from waging his disastrous war. Would the U.S.A. be in a stronger position today if Hussein's Iraq really *had* been bristling with operational nuclear weapons? At least that would have prevented Bush from wasting 5 trillion dollars and squandering America's reputation on an ever-deepening quagmire.

Respected journalist Ron Suskind has confirmed that Bush was informed by his intelligence community that Iraq had no WMD. Bush, knowing full well that Iraq had no WMD, lied to America and to the world.[150]

Hard, absolute, undeniable proof that the Bush Administration lied America into war has existed ever since the Downing Street Memo was published on May 1st, 2005.[151]

Astonishingly, Bush even ordered the CIA to forge and backdate a bogus handwritten document linking al-Qaeda to Saddam Hussein in order to create a false pretext for his illegal war of aggression against Iraq![152]

Despite this cold, hard proof that the Iraq war was launched on lies, the neocons have continued to claim that the Iraq invasion had something to do with the "War on Terror." As Bush himself said, "We are fighting these terrorists with our military in Afghanistan and Iraq and beyond so we do not have to face them in the streets of our own cities."[153] Former terror czar Richard Clarke points out the problem with Bush's logic: "Of course, nothing about our being 'over there' in any way prevents terrorists from coming here. Quite the opposite, the evidence is overwhelming that our presence provides motivation for people throughout the Arab world to become anti-American terrorists."[154]

The official conspiracy theory—which holds that Bush invaded Iraq in order to "fight terrorism"— does not fare well in its battle with the facts.

Everybody's Favorite Conspiracy Theory: Was the Iraq Invasion Really About Oil?

Is it just a coincidence that the U.S. invaded Iraq—which has the largest untapped and unmapped reserves of sweet crude oil in the world—rather than one of the dozens of countries with nasty regimes but no oil? Is that a rhetorical question or what?

But would U.S. leaders dream of doing such a thing? Is the Pope Catholic? Is Cheney from Haliburton?

Even Jimmy Carter, who was not exactly a hard-line militarist, made it absolutely clear that the U.S. would happily invade for oil. In 1979 he formulated the Carter Doctrine, which says the United States will use military force to maintain access to Middle Eastern oil. The Carter Doctrine has been official U.S. policy since 1979.

Back in 1975, Henry Kissinger, writing under the pseudonym "Miles Ignotus" (Latin for 'unknown soldier') authored an article entitled "Seizing Arab Oil."[155] Published in *Harper's*, Kissinger's article argued that the Arab-heavy oil cartel OPEC posed a threat that could only be countered by military force. The article advocated a surprise U.S. invasion of Saudi Arabia and the seizure of Saudi oil fields. As Kissinger famously put it, "Oil is much too important a commodity to be left in the hands of the Arabs."[156]

The Carter Doctrine, and Kissinger's quote and article, suggest that the U.S. government *would* invade the Middle East in order to seize its oilfields. But *did* that actually happen when the U.S. invaded Iraq?

Plenty of evidence suggests that the answer is "yes." Oil expert Richard Heinberg puts it bluntly: "The U.S. invasion of Iraq is clearly a resource war."[157] In his paper "Oil Interests and the U.S. Invasion of Iraq," Professor Hassan El-Najjar explains:

> Islamic countries generally, and Arab states in particular, have been blessed with a huge oil wealth most of which is still stored underground. The total proven Arab oil reserves amount to about 592 billion barrels (bb). According to EIA, Saudi Arabia has the largest reserves (259 bb), followed by Iraq (100 bb), UAE (96.5 bb), Kuwait (94 bb), Libya (29.5), Algeria (9.2 bb), and Qatar (3.7 bb). Using the beginning of the year 2000 oil prices of about $25 per barrel, the Arab oil wealth may be estimated at about $14.8 trillion. However, this figure is expected to be much higher because oil prices are more likely to increase throughout the 21st century. Because oil is a finite resource, it becomes scarcer with more use. Therefore, its prices are more likely to become higher.[158]

They may already have. Since Dr. El-Najjar presented his paper, the value of that Arab oil rose from roughly 15 trillion dollars to more than 50 trillion dollars. At those prices, Iraq's reserves, which conservative estimates put at about one-sixth of the total Arab oil reserves, will be worth more than 10 trillion dollars. In fact, Iraq may have far more oil than that. Of all the Arab countries, Iraq holds the most promise of further discoveries. Some think Iraq has more reserves than Saudi Arabia:

> A new book written by a team of experts provides a field-by-field detailed explication of the thesis that Iraqi oil reserves are substantially greater than previously thought. The proven reserves were officially put at 112 billion barrels in 2007 but the final figure could exceed 300 billion barrels.[159]

If true, this means Iraq's oil wealth in is worth more than 30 *trillion* dollars as of this writing—and those prices are expected to rise sharply in the near future, and keep right on rising. Can anybody seriously argue that such unimaginable oil wealth was not a factor in Bush's invasion of Iraq—especially if the Saudi oilfields are largely played out, as Matt Simmons argues?[160]

Many analysts, including Heinberg, say it's even more serious than that. They argue—and statistics seem to bear them out—that global demand for oil is outstripping supply. The world of the future will never have enough oil to meet demand. The world economy is in for a series of oil shocks, maybe even a "long emergency" that will not end for generations, if at all.[161]

But is there any concrete evidence that Bush and Cheney had oil on their minds when they drew up their plan to invade Iraq?

Hell, yes.

Bush's original Treasury Secretary, Paul O'Neill, has informed us that the Bush Administration began planning the invasion of Iraq in January, 2001—half a year before 9/11. According to O'Neill, from the moment the Bush Administration took office, Rumsfeld and Wolfowitz began laying out the case for invading Iraq, and Bush responded "Fine. Go find me a way to do this."[162] By February 2001, "hard-liners like Rumsfeld, Cheney and Wolfowitz" were "already planning the next war in Iraq and the shape of a post-Saddam country."[163] Simultaneously, according to O'Neill, "Documents were being prepared by the Defense Intelligence Agency, Rumsfeld's intelligence arm, mapping Iraq's oil fields and exploration areas and listing companies that might be interested in leveraging the precious asset."[164] One such document mapped

Iraq "with markings for 'supergiant oilfield,' 'other oilfield,' and 'earmarked for production sharing,' while demarking the largely undeveloped southwest of the country into nine 'blocks' to designate areas for future exploration."[165] In short, within a month of taking power, the Bush Administration had already decided to invade Iraq, mapping out that unsuspecting nation to be carved up for oil like a cow scheduled for butchering might be carved up for its meat.

The lion's share was apportioned to Cheney's friends at Haliburton. According to journalist Jason Leopold:

> Four months before the United States invaded Iraq, the Department of Defense was secretly working with Vice Pesident Dick Cheney's old company, Halliburton Corp. on a secret deal that would give the world's second largest oil services company total control over Iraq's oil fields, according to interviews with Halliburton's most senior executives.
>
> Previously undisclosed Halliburton documents obtained by The Public Record confirm that controlling the world's second largest oil reserves was a top priority for the Bush administration. Additionally, the deal between the Department of Defense and Halliburton unit Kellogg, Brown & Root to operate Iraq's oil industry saved Halliburton from imminent bankruptcy.[166]

After the invasion and occupation, did the U.S. impose an enlightened oil policy designed to rebuild Iraq and put oil profits into that nation's education and infrastructure? Hardly. After setting up a quisling puppet government, the U.S. occupiers rammed through a law, unbeknownst to most of the quisling lawmakers themselves, that "gives foreign corporations access to almost every sector of Iraq's oil and natural gas industry."[167]

Naomi Klein, author of *The Shock Doctrine: The Rise of Disaster Capitalism*, describes the Iraq oil grab as "the greatest stick-up in history."[168] She deplores the "no-bid service contracts announced for Exxon Mobil, Chevron, Shell, BP and Total... While ostensibly under the control of the Iraq National Oil Company, foreign corporations will keep 75% of the value of the contracts, leaving just 25% for their Iraqi partners. That kind of ratio is unheard of in oil-rich Arab and Persian states, where achieving majority national control over oil was the defining victory of anti-colonial struggles."[169]

Klein adds:

> Several of the architects of the Iraq war no longer even bother to deny that oil was a major motivator for the invasion. On U.S. National Public Radio's To the Point, Fadhil Chalabi, one of the primary Iraqi advisers to the Bush administration in the lead-up to the invasion, recently described the war as "a strategic move on the part of the United States of America and the UK to have a military presence in the Gulf in order to secure [oil] supplies in the future." Chalabi, who served as Iraq's oil undersecretary of state and met with the oil majors before the invasion, described this as "a primary objective."[170]

We now know that Iraq never posed a threat to Americans. It had no WMDs, and no connection whatsoever to any terrorist attacks in the United States. Given the facts we have just reviewed, "stealing oil" seems a more probable motive for the Iraq invasion than "fighting terror."

There is, however, a surprisingly strong argument that the Terror Wars cannot have been motivated by oil. The crux of this argument is that oil markets have been fully globalized, so it doesn't really matter who "owns" the oil. According to this argument, sellers are going to sell to buyers at a price determined not by the owner of the oil, but by a combination of global market forces and the skullduggery of the global financiers, who sometimes manage to rig the global markets, at least temporarily. According to those who argue against WFO (war for oil) the big oil companies never wanted the war, which they knew would not serve their interests.

Cyrus Bina writes:

> The war-for-oil scenario, as a popular myth, ignores the deeper understanding of the complex web of contradictions and regulating dynamics of today's economy and polity. Yet, the very anachronism of this scenario is understandable in the view of the anachronistic U.S. behavior that is so dreadfully attempting to reverse the loss of American hegemony against time and, more importantly, history. Therefore, parallel with

the anachronistic reality of U.S. colonial conduct in Iraq, the anachronism of the "oil grab" becomes "reality" in the minds of those who chant "No Blood for Oil." Yet, holding a parallel between the U.S. invasion of Iraq and the control of oil is a far-fetched proposition, if not an outright illusion. For, since the mid-1970s, the material bases and dynamics of post-cartelization and globalization of oil render the physical access, prearranged inter-company allocation, and indeed administrative control and pricing of oil redundant. This rather counter intuitive reality also renders any connection between the war and oil—other than given disbursement to finance matters such as the establishment of a puppet government—superfluous.[171]

James Petras adds:

The major advocates of the 'war for oil' (WFO) argument fail several empirical tests: Namely that the oil companies were not actively supporting the war via propaganda, congressional lobbying or through any other policy vehicle. Secondly the proponents of WFO fail to explain the efforts by major oil companies to develop economic ties with Iraq prior to the invasion and were in fact, working through clandestine third parties to trade in Iraqi oil. Thirdly, all the major oil companies operating in the Middle East were mainly concerned with political stability, the liberalization of the economic policies of the region and the opening of oil services for foreign investors... Not a single CEO from the entire petroleum industry viewed the US invasion as a positive 'national security' measure... Moreover the oil companies had several real prospects of developing lucrative service and commercial oil contracts with Saddam Hussein's regime in the lead-up to the war. It was the US government pressured by the Zionist Power Configuration (ZPC), which pushed legislation blocking (through sanctions) Big Oil from consummating these economic agreements with Iraq... Despite the war, liberalization elsewhere in the region has proceeded and US oil and financial interests have advanced despite the increased obstacles and hostilities, which have grown out of the US slaughter of Muslims...

If oil was not the real motive, then what was?

Petras again:

> There is an alternative view which argues that Israel promoted the US attack on Iraq, did all in its power through its US pro-Israel followers to design, propagandize and plan the war. This alternative view sustains that at no point did the Zion-Cons act contrary to Israeli state interests. In fact, Israeli officials worked on a daily basis with its US agents inside the government, particularly the Pentagon's Office of Special Plans to provide disinformation to justify the military attack. If, as we will show, Israel was deeply involved in pushing the US to attack Iraq and is behind the current disinformation campaign to provoke a US war against Iran, then anti-war forces and US public opinion must openly confront the 'Israel factor'.

> We will argue that the exoneration of Israel is mainly an attempt to deflect US public hostility away from those Israel Firsters who manipulated us into this costly, bloody unending war.[172]

Zelikow's Conspiracy Theory: Was the Iraq War Really a Disguised War for Israel?

Despite the ever-receding horizon of lucrative future oil profits, the Iraq war has been a disaster for the U.S.A., as all informed experts predicted it would be. But, as Netanyahu continues to brag, it has been a triumph for Israel.[173] All of this was completely predictable and widely known by experts even before the war started. Given all of this, we are forced to ask: Did pro-Israel forces help orchestrate the war?

Prior to the U.S. invasion of Iraq, Saddam Hussein's government had been supporting the Palestinian resistance against Israeli occupation. Most famously, Hussein had been providing generous sums for the families of martyrs who died fighting the Israelis. Thanks in part to help from Iraq, the Palestinian intifada had been successfully damaging the Israeli economy by scaring away tourists and would-be immigrants. The Palestinians had even equalized the casualty ratio to a certain extent. Before the Iraq invasion, "only" five Palestinians were being killed for each Israeli death.

The Israelis were being forced to taste at least a small portion of the suffering they were inflicting. After the invasion, Iraqi aid disappeared, and the Israelis were able to massacre Palestinians at will; the casualty ratio grew to dozens of Palestinians killed for each Israeli death.

Did Zionists manipulate the U.S. into invading Iraq? We have seen that the neoconservatives, most of whom are U.S.-Israeli dual citizens, wrote the script for the Iraq war in 1995 with their *Clean Break* statement, which was commissioned by Israeli Prime Minister Netanyahu. Then these same Zionist neoconservative minions of Netanyahu swept into power when Bush stole the 2000 election. Perle, Feith, Wurmsur, Wolfowitz, Libby, Fleischer—all Zionist fanatics! These were the people who took over U.S. foreign policy in 2001. As a senior Bush Administration official told the Washington Post in 2003, "The Likudniks are really in charge now."[174] (Israel's extremist Likud Party is the party of Netanyahu and Ariel Sharon.)

Another senior Bush Administration official actually admitted that the U.S. invasion of Iraq had nothing to do with U.S. security, but was really about the threat "that dare not speak its name"—the threat to Israel. That official was Philip Zelikow, then a member of the President's Foreign Intelligence Advisory Board (PFIAB), which reports directly to the president. Before that, Zelikow was part of Bush's transition team, and co-authored a book with Condoleeza Rice. Zelikow later became the czar of the 9/11 Commission and, essentially, the sole author of the *9/11 Commission Report*. As we have seen, Zelikow, whose academic speciality is the creation and maintenance of public myths based "searing or moulding" events, appears to have had foreknowledge of the 9/11 attacks.

Here are Zelikow's own words during a September 10, 2002 speech at the University of Virginia:

"Why would Iraq attack America or use nuclear weapons against us? I'll tell you what I think the real threat (is) and actually has been since 1990—it's the threat against Israel. And this is the threat that dare not speak its name, because the Europeans don't care deeply about that threat, I will tell you frankly. And the American government doesn't wasnt to lean too hard on it rhetorically, because it is not a popular sell."[175]

Did Zelikow—himself a pro-Zionist Jew—let the cat out of the bag?

Many well-informed Americans think so. James Petras, a widely-respected sociology professor who has published more than 60 books in 29 languages along with over 560 scholarly articles, argues that the Jewish lobby has a stranglehold over U.S. Middle East policy.[176] Petras is now calling for an "American national liberation struggle" to free the U.S.A. from Zionist rule.[177]

Time Magazine columnist Joe Klein, himself Jewish and pro-Israel, writes: "The fact that a great many Jewish neoconservatives — people like Joe Lieberman and the crowd over at Commentary — plumped for this (Iraq) war, and now for an even more foolish assault on Iran, raised the question of divided loyalties: using U.S. military power, U.S. lives and money, to make the world safe for Israel." After the predictable squeals from the neocons, Klein fired back: "You want evidence of divided loyalties? How about the 'benign domino theory' that so many Jewish neoconservatives talked to me about—off the record, of course—in the runup to the Iraq war, the idea that Israel's security could be won by taking out Saddam, which would set off a cascade of disaster for Israel's enemies in the region? As my grandmother would say, feh! Do you actually deny that the casus belli that dare not speak its name wasn't, as I wrote in February 2003, a desire to make the world safe for Israel? Why the rush now to bomb Iran, a country that poses some threat to Israel but none—for the moment—to the United States...unless we go ahead, attack it, and the mullahs unleash Hezbollah terrorists against us?"[178]

Former CIA analysts Bill and Kathleen Christison, in their 2003 article "Too Many Smoking Guns to Ignore: Israel, American Jews, and the War on Iraq" made the same point. So have dozens of other respected analysts.

Could Zelikow, the author of the government's official conspiracy theory of 9/11, be correct in his assertion that the Iraq war was a Zionist conspiracy? If he is correct, were those who pushed us into a war on behalf of another country with which we are not even allied guilty of treason against the United States of America? (Israel is not a U.S. ally; it refuses to enter into any alliance with the U.S. because if it did, it would have to declare official borders.)[179]

These are questions that deserve serious thought and investigation.

Is the War on Terror Orwellian?

The adjective *Orwellian* refers to the political vision of one of the 20th century's greatest writers, George Orwell, especially as he expressed that vision in his dystopian novel *1984*. Specifically, it describes a government, society, or specific policies using:

• **The twisting of language for political purposes, especially when the resulting violations of meaning are outrageous yet unnoticed.** Examples from *1984* include the party slogans *war is peace, freedom is slavery, and ignorance is strength.* Orwell especially targets official uses of language to downplay or eliminate meanings and ideas that threaten the ruling elite. Examples from the War on Terror include using *extraordinary rendition* for state-sanctioned kidnapping and torture; *collateral damage* to mean the foreseeable, and thus intentional, mass slaughter of civilians; *conspiracy theorist* to insult those who claim the rulers have done something gravely wrong and should be held accountable; *terrorist* to refer to anyone the rulers consider their enemy; *pre-emptive war* for unprovoked and illegal war of aggression; *National Security* for policies designed to make people fearful and insecure; *they hate our freedoms* as a catch-all phrase for the supposed motives of real and alleged "terrorists"; and of course the *War on Terror* itself, which is actually a war *of* terror against the domestic population as well as the foreign "enemy."

• **Worshipping the rulers**. After 9/11 and the declaration of the "War on Terror," Bush's popularity shot up to almost 90%. It was a genuinely Orwellian moment. Bush was still being worshipped six months later even though he had retreated from his promise to get Bin Laden dead or alive by saying "I truly am not that concerned about him."

• **Doublethink**: Accepting outrageous contradictions from the rulers without even noticing. One obvious example was just mentioned: Bush vowing to "get Bin Laden dead or alive" and then saying "I truly am not that concerned about him." Another example is the imagined opposition between liberty and freedom, as in "we must sacrifice some of our freedom in order to preserve our liberty." The idea that we should respond to an alleged attack by those who "hate our freedom" by *getting rid of* some of our freedom might also be viewed as Orwellian doublethink. Attacking Iraq as a response to 9/11, when Iraq had nothing to do with 9/11, also required a dollop of doublethink—and seven out of ten Americans complied, accepting a completely imaginary link between Saddam Hussein and 9/11.[180] In 2006, after everyone, including the Bush Administration, had admitted that there was no such link, nearly half of the American public still believed in the fiction.[181]

- **Replacing the family with government as the source of authority and reassurance in a frightening world.** Orwell's dystopian government was personalized as "Big Brother." Your big brother is the guy who defends you if you're attacked, who saves you if you're in trouble, and who has a certain natural authority over you. Even if he doesn't always treat you as well as he should, you don't mind too much because you love him. (Orwell's novel ends with "He loved Big Brother.")

The War on Terror began on the date 9/11—the same digits as 911, the number we are told to dial if we're in serious trouble. Instead of turning to a family member for help, by dialing 911 we turn to the imaginary father figure of the government. A high percentage of 911 calls actually involve calling the government for help *against* a family member—a symptom of the breakdown in the family in today's society, and the rampant substitution of government authority for family and community solidarity.

When our biggest national emergency ever happened on 9/11, we were immediately brainwashed by surrogate parent figures, the TV newscasters, who directed us to look to our ultimate father figure for salvation. And that ultimate father figure was not God, but the government—especially the president, who since the days of Washington has been the symbolic "father of his country." Bush's popularity soared to 90% because he became the father (or big brother) to whom we turn for help in time of need. The fact that the emergency had happened on 9/11, the same three numbers as the emergency call number 911, cemented that psychological relationship. If someone had wanted to make Americans feel an Orwellian love for Big Brother in Washington, D.C., they could not have picked a better method than to conduct a spectacular, nationally-televised terrorist attack on the eleventh of September.

• **Rampant violations of personal privacy.** In Orwell's *1984*, the government is everywhere, even spying on people in their own living rooms through their TV sets! Obviously Orwell's dystopia has no Fourth Amendment. Neither, unfortunately, does the post-War on Terror USA.

The Fourth Amendment of the US Constitution reads: "The right of the people to be secure in their persons, houses, papers, and effects, against unreasonable searches and seizures, shall not be violated, and no Warrants shall issue, but upon probable cause, supported by Oath or affirmation, and particularly describing the place to be searched, and the persons or things to be seized."

That's as clear as it could possibly get. The Fourth Amendment explains precisely what the government may and may not do: It may search citizens and/or seize property *if and only if* the authorities obtain a search warrant specifically ("particularly") describing exactly what they are looking for, where, and why. In the absence of such a warrant, the authorities may not search anyone or seize anything.[182] Since this restriction applied to all forms of remote communication (the mail) when the Constitution was ratified in 1789, it obviously still applies to all forms of remote communication today: phone calls, emails, faxes, and so on.

But even before 9/11 officially launched the "War on Terror," Bush had thrown the Fourth Amendment out the window. According to mainstream media sources, "The U.S. National Security Agency asked AT&T Inc. to help it set up a domestic call monitoring site seven months before the Sept. 11, 2001 attacks, lawyers claimed June 23 in court papers filed in New York federal court."[183]

The National Security Agency (NSA) is prohibited by law from spying on people within the USA. That didn't stop Bush from ordering the NSA to start spying on Americans seven months before 9/11. NSA whisteblower Wayne Madsen has reported that the real reason for the spying had nothing to do with "National Security." Instead, Bush ordered NSA to dig up dirt on his political opponents.[184] Why would he risk such a blatantly illegal operation

68

seven months before 9/11, when the next presidential election was still almost four years away? So he would be in a position to blackmail anyone who threatened to speak the truth about what was coming?

In a further demonstration of Orwellianism, Congress retroactively granted both Bush and the telecoms complete immunity from prosecution for their outrageous crimes against privacy and the Constitution. The 2008 FISA Bill, passed by both Houses of Congress and approved by many Democrats including Obama, not only kept the treasonous telecom executives out of jail, but also effectively abolished the Fourth Amendment, according to leading Constitutional scholar Jonathan Turley.[185]

Senator Frank Church (D-Idaho) saw it coming back in 1975 when he wrote: "I don't want to see this country ever go across the bridge. I know the capacity that is there to make tyranny total in America, and we must see to it that this agency [the National Security Agency] and all agencies that possess this technology operate within the law and under proper supervision, so that we never cross over that abyss. That is the abyss from which there is no return."[186]

Even back in 1975, the Stone Age of surveillance technology compared to today, the NSA had the ability to impose absolute and complete remote surveillance of every single US citizen so that there would be "no place to hide" and "no way to fight back." As Senator Church put it, "that capability at any time could be turned around on the American people, and no American would have any privacy left, such is the capability to monitor everything: telephone conversations, telegrams, it doesn't matter. There would be no place to hide. . . . There would be no way to fight back because the most careful effort to combine together in resistance to the government, no matter how privately it was done, is within the reach of the government to know."[187]

Are we already living in the age of total tyranny that Senator Church warned us against? Is the tyranny that much worse because most of us don't realize it? In short, is today's USA already far beyond Orwell's worst nightmare? (Even in the dystopian world of *1984* a degree of privacy is available, at least temporarily, when one is out of reach of the living room spy camera.)

• **The forced forgetting of history, and the widespread acceptance of whatever version of history the rulers are promoting at the moment.** At the beginning of *1984,* "we are at war with Eurasia. We have always been at war with Eurasia." Halfway through the book, the rulers suddenly claim: "We are at war with Eastasia. We have always been at war with Eastasia. Eurasia is our ally." The population accepts this matter-of-factly, just as most Americans matter-of-factly accepted that they were now-and-ever at war with Iraq rather than al-Qaeda in 2003, and then Iran (an ally against both Saddam Hussein's Iraq and the Taliban's Afghanistan) in 2007. In 2008, America's Orwellian rulers squabbled about whether Iran would continue to be the designated arch-enemy, or whether that title would be bestowed upon Pakistan, Russia, and/or (eventually) China, yet most people hardly noticed the confusion.

The number of mainstream-media-reported facts about the 9/11 attacks themselves that have been forcibly forgotten is astounding. An extensive collection of forcibly-forgotten facts concerning 9/11, reported once by the media and then obliterated from collective memory, may be found in Paul Thompson's *The Terror Timeline.*[188] We will examine a few of these forgotten facts in Part Two of this book.

• **A dystopian future.** The "War on Terror," like Orwell's dystopia, promises a war that cannot possibly ever end. Dick Cheney aptly called it "The war that will not end in our lifetime." Neocon ex-CIA Director James Woolsey has called it "World War IV."[189] Woolsey sees it continuing indefinitely: "This fourth world war, I think, will last considerably longer than either World Wars I or II did for us."[190] As we have seen, this endless war against an abstract noun has eviscerated civil liberties, introduced radical new forms of mass mind control, beggared the economy, desensitized the public to the use of extreme violence and torture against innocent people, replaced a government of public servants and a society of family values with Big Brother, and largely eliminated truth from public discourse. *1984* was written in 1948, and to most people then, *1984* seemed a lot worse than 1948. Is post-2001 actually worse than *1984*? Has the War on Terror ushered in a world where things just keep getting worse and worse...forever?

Part Two:
Case Studies in Questionable Terrorism

The word *terrorism* conjures up images of mindless, pointless violence, perpetrated by crazed fanatics without any realistic goals. But the vast majority of terrorist acts, and virtually all of the big ones, are committed by disciplined cadres, whether in or out of uniform, in pursuit of specific military objectives.

Many military tactics can be classified as terrorism. For example, if "terrorism" means "intentional violence against civilians designed to instill fear," the US nuclear bombings of Hiroshima and Nagasaki were probably the biggest acts of terrorism ever committed. From a military-strategic standpoint, the terrorist bombings of Hiroshima and Nagasaki were quite successful, at least in the short run. They terrorized the Japanese into unconditional surrender. And they terrorized the Russians into letting the US have its way in Europe, despite the huge US conventional military disadvantage.

Most terrorist bombings are not nearly as big and successful. But they are just as calculating and strategic.

Robert Pape's *Dying to Win: The Strategic Logic of Suicide Terrorism* explains that suicide terrorism is a logical weapon-of-last-resort for occupied peoples to use against their occupiers. It is a way for occupied peoples to increase the cost of occupation to the point that the occupier finally gives up and goes home. Pape points out that "what nearly all suicide terrorist attacks have in common is a specific secular and strategic goal: to compel modern democracies to withdraw military forces from territory that the terrorists consider to be their homeland."[191] Pape's book suggests that if war is the terrorism of the strong, terrorism is the warfare of the weak.

Small-scale insurgent groups normally take credit for their acts, issuing threats and demands in the immediate aftermath of the violence they have perpetrated. In most cases, the identity and goals of the perpetrators of any given attack are obvious from the get-go.

However, in the case of some terrorist attacks—often the biggest, most spectacular ones—questions arise about who really did it, and why. Sometimes these questions are answered fairly quickly. Other times they persist indefinitely.

In this section, we will examine questions surrounding various terrorist incidents, beginning with the Gunpowder Plot and continuing through today's War on Terror.

Who Were the Real Gunpowder Plotters?

"Remember, remember the Fifth of November, the gunpowder treason and plot. I see no reason why gunpowder treason should ever be forgot."

The movie *V for Vendetta*, even more than the graphic novel that inspired it, is based on the most spectacular terrorist failure in history: the Gunpowder Plot of 1605.

The Gunpowder Plot had a momentous impact on British public opinion. Even today, 400 years later, people in Britain and the Commonwealth countries commemorate the failure of the plot every November 5th, Guy Fawkes Day, by hanging or burning lead plotter Guy Fawkes in effigy (or lighting symbolic bonfires) and setting off fireworks.

Wikipedia offers the standard version of the 1605 Gunpowder Plot:

> The Gunpowder Plot of 1605, or the Powder Treason, as it was known at the time, was a failed assassination attempt by a group of provincial English Catholics against King James I of England and VI of Scotland. The plot intended to kill the king, his family, and most of the Protestant aristocracy in a single attack by blowing up the Houses of Parliament during the State Opening on 5 November 1605... Some popular historians have put forward a debate about government involvement in the plot.[192]

According to the official version, the plot blew up in the face of the Catholic plotters when the gunpowder they had hauled to the basement of Parliament did not blow up. Instead, the plotters and their gunpowder were seized, and a thunderous government propaganda operation commenced. Catholics were demonized, persecutions were launched, and Britain began a century of warfare with two key Catholic powers, France and Spain. Because of its effect on British public opinion, which enabled the subsequent century of war, the Gunpowder Plot may have been the most important geopolitical event of the 17th century, if not the whole modern era. The fizzling-out of the Gunpowder Plot was the explosion that launched the British Empire.

Some historians, beginning with the Jesuit scholar John Gerard (1564-1606), have argued that the official story of the Gunpowder Plot is "well-nigh incredible," and that the British government must have known exactly what the plotters were up to.[193] Some go further and blame the plot on a faction of the British government, the "war party" led by Lord Robert Cecil. Webster Tarpley explains that Cecil and his hawkish cabal opposed the policies of King James, who was making peace with Spain and supporting toleration for English Catholics. Cecil's War Party, by contrast was whipping up anti-Catholic sentiment and pushing for an attack on Catholic Spain—a war from which they planned to make a lot of money, and in the event were not disappointed.

Tarpley explains the plot-behind-the-plot :

> Acting behind the scenes, Cecil cultivated some prominent Catholics, one of them Lord Thomas Percy from the famous Catholic Percy family, and used them as cut-outs to direct the operations of a group of naive Catholic fanatics and adventurers, among them a certain gullible gentleman named Guy Fawkes. Thomas Percy was supposedly a Catholic fanatic, but in reality was a bigamist. This group of Catholic fanatics hatched the idea first of tunneling into the basement of the Houses of Parliament from a nearby house, and then simply of renting the basement of the Houses of Parliament, in order to pack that basement with explosives for the purpose of blowing up Kings, Lords, and Commons when King James I came to open the Parliament early that November. But instead Guy Fawkes was caught going into the basement the night before the great crime was scheduled to occur. Fawkes and the rest of the plotters were tortured and hanged and several Catholic clergy were also scapegoated. James I put aside his plans of toleration of Catholics, and England set out on a century of wars against

the Spanish and Portuguese Empires, from which in turn the British Empire was born.[194]

If the interpretation suggested by Gerard, Nicolson, Tarpley, Zwicker, Williamson, and others is correct, the Gunpowder Plot is the prototype of what Tarpley and others call *state-sponsored false-flag terror*. According to this version, the Plot was state-sponsored in that it was guided by a faction of plotters in the English government. And it was a false-flag operation in that the real force behind the operation, the War Party, did not advertise itself. Instead, it blamed the plot on its Catholic enemies, and successfully convinced the British people, and much of the world, to do so as well.

Was the Gunpowder Plot a classic case of state-sponsored false-flag terror? Have mainstream historians honestly considered this question? Are British historians inevitably biased in favor of the official British government version of such events? Can genuinely critical historians correct for this bias and successfully revise official history? Just how important a historical role is played by acts of state-sponsored false-flag terror? Can whole empires be built on single, spectacular false-flag terror episodes? Whatever the ultimate answers, the Gunpowder Plot revisionists raise some interesting questions.

Who Blew Up the *Maine?*

"Remember the Maine, to hell with Spain!"

Just as the British Empire was built on anti-Catholic feeling whipped up by the Gunpowder Plot, the USA's overseas empire was made possible by anti-Spanish hysteria triggered by the sinking of the battleship *Maine* on February 15th, 1898. (It's interesting that both Britain and the US built their empires by demonizing and attacking Spain.)

William Randolph Hearst's yellow journalism led the way in blaming the Spanish. But today, the real cause of the sinking of the *Maine* remains a mystery. About the only thing historians agree on is that whoever or whatever may have caused the *Maine*'s demise, it definitely wasn't an intentional attack by Spain. The Spanish were militarily far weaker than the U.S. and had no reason to want to start a war. They knew the US could use the outbreak of war as an excuse to steal what remained of their empire. And in the event, that was exactly what happened.

The official story of the sinking of the *Maine* is that we will never really know why it blew up. Amazingly, this official story was already in place the day after the event! On February 16th, 1898, Assistant Secretary to the Navy Theodore Rooscvclt was clairvoyantly insisting that "we shall never find out definitely" what had happened to the *Maine* the day before.[195] How could he possibly have known that?

Shortly before the sinking of the *Maine*, journalist-illustrator Frederic Remington, who had been sent to Havana by William Randolph Hearst to cover alleged Spanish atrocities that would lead to war with the US, sent Hearst the news that there were no atrocities and no signs of impending war. Hearst famously replied: "You furnish the pictures and I'll furnish the war."[196] While the quote may be apocryphal, and Hearst obviously cannot have personally blown up the *Maine*, it does suggest that those around Hearst thought that Hearst had foreknowledge of the impending disaster and the hostilities it would trigger (just as Teddy Roosevelt had foreknowledge that no amount of investigation would ever ascertain what happened to the *Maine*).

Another suspicious fact about the explosion aboard the *Maine* is that it targeted the ship's forequarters, where the enlisted men were housed, sparing the officers, who were quartered in the aft section of the ship. Of the two hundred and sixty-six men who died in or immediately after the explosion, and the eight more who died later from injuries, virtually none were officers. Captain Charles Sigsbee and almost all the *Maine*'s officers survived—just as Rumsfeld and the rest of the top brass survived the attack on the Pentagon on 9/11, which conveniently targeted the section of the Pentagon that was furthest from their offices.

The various investigations of the *Maine* disaster, like the two official investigations of the murder of JFK, have offered contradictory accounts.[197] The first investigation was by a U.S. Naval Board of Inquiry dispatched to Havana shortly after the incident. The Board of Inquiry determined that the ship had been destroyed by the explosion of a stash of ammunition magazines in the forequarters of the ship. It claimed that the explosion was triggered by an external blast such as a mine. This conclusion provided ammunition for the proponents of war with Spain. Another Naval Court of Inquiry, held in 1911, essentially parroted the findings of the 1898 Board.

Subsequent investigations, however, have cast doubt on those findings. A thorough investigation by Admiral Hyman G. Rickover and a team of Navy scientists in 1976 concluded that the cause of the explosion originated inside the ship, not outside it. Bound by the strictures of political correctness, Admiral Rickover did not even mention the most obvious possibility: intentional sabotage designed to provoke an avidly-desired war with Spain. Admitting that the cause of the internal explosion could not be determined, he offered the hypothesis that the culprit might have been a coal bunker fire.

Despite his polite refusal to voice what everybody was thinking, Rickover's 1976 investigation posed an obvious threat to the triumphalist, see-no-evil version of U.S. history. Rickover's finding that the *Maine* had been blown up from within came during the post-Watergate 1976-1978 period that saw Congress investigating CIA abuses and political assassinations. The Rickover report contributed to an atmosphere of growing skepticism about the Gulf of Tonkin incident, Pearl Harbor, and other spectacular war trigger events.

In 1999, the U.S. was, unbeknownst to most Americans, on the brink of the War on Terror and the spectacular 9/11 attacks that would launch it. Rickover's "internal explosion" theory of the Maine's demise posed an inconvenience, lest Americans put two and two together, re-think the standard accounts of Pearl Harbor and the *Maine*, and begin to suspect that their own government was capable of murdering large numbers of innocent Americans in order to stampede the nation into avidly-desired wars.

Conveniently for those who fear public skepticism, in 1999 the National Geographic Society commissioned an inquiry by an outfit calling itself Advanced Marine Enterprises. The new study undertook the task of casting doubt on Rickover's conclusions. While forced to admit that it could not definitely say that the explosion had been external, AME argued that "it appears more probable than was previously concluded" that a mine was to blame.

Since Rickover had concluded that the probability of a mine was very low, while the probability of an internal cause was very high, even a small possibility that a mine was to blame would make that explanation "more probable than was previously concluded." In short, A.M.E. damns its own hypothesis with faint praise. But by using such deceptive phrasing, it was able to sow doubt about Rickover's conclusions, and thereby keep the "false-flag inside job" interpretation of the *Maine* one step removed from public consciousness.

When we keep in mind that U.S. expansionists like Roosevelt, Hearst, and the rest of the War Party were desperately looking for a *causus belli* to launch their war with Spain, it seems reasonable to ask whether the sinking of the *Maine* was a classic case of state-sponsored false-flag terrorism.

Did U.S. Military Terrorists Plan a False-Flag "Attack on America" in 1962?

Amazingly enough, the answer to this question appears to be an unequivocal "yes." A 2001 ABC News report broke the news to the American public:

> In the early 1960s, America's top military leaders reportedly drafted plans to kill innocent people and commit acts of terrorism in U.S. cities to create public support for a war against Cuba.
>
> Code named Operation Northwoods, the plans reportedly included the possible assassination of Cuban émigrés, sinking boats of Cuban refugees on the high seas, hijacking planes, blowing up a U.S. ship, and even orchestrating violent terrorism in U.S. cities.
>
> The plans were developed as ways to trick the American public and the international community into supporting a war to oust Cuba's then new leader, communist Fidel Castro.
>
> America's top military brass even contemplated causing U.S. military casualties, writing: "We could blow up a U.S. ship in Guantanamo Bay and blame Cuba," and, "casualty lists in U.S. newspapers would cause a helpful wave of national indignation."[198]

The revelation came in James Bamford's book *Body of Secrets*, published less than five months before 9/11.[199] Bamford is considered the unofficial house biographer of the National Security Agency, America's biggest intelligence agency. Bamford's sources included a preserved copy of the original Operation Northwoods document proposing the plan. Amazingly, the document was signed by General Lyman Lemnitzer, then the head of the Joint Chiefs of Staff, along with every other member of the Joint Chiefs. *Every single member of the Joint Chiefs of Staff signed this document calling for the mass murder of US citizens in acts of false-flag state-sponsored terrorism.*[200]

If it hadn't been for Oliver Stone's film *JFK* we would probably never know that Operation Northwoods had ever existed. The success of Stone's 1991 film, and the controversy it provoked, led Congress to pass the JFK Act of 1992, which created the John F. Kennedy Assassination Records Review Board and "required agencies that held assassination records to record information about these records on Record Identification Forms (RIFs) for input into a master database" and made public.[201] The previously secret Operation Northwoods document was first made public in November, 1997, by the JFK Review Board.

What did Operation Northwoods have to do with the JFK assassination? The question remains open. JFK's arch-enemy, ultra-hawk Joint Chiefs Chairman Lyman Lemnitzer, drew up the Northwoods plan and sent it to Kennedy for approval. Kennedy (through Robert MacNamara) rejected the plan and fired Lemnitzer. Some historians argue that Kennedy's firing of such hard-liners as false-flag terrormeister Lemnitzer and CIA Chief Allen Dulles, and his turn toward peace and disarmament, sealed his fate.[202] Was it sheer coincidence that Kennedy's plan to withdraw from Vietnam was reversed just two days after his assassination?[203]

Did U.S. Military Terrorists Stage False-Flag Terror Attacks on Innocent Civilians in Europe During the Cold War?

From the 1960s through through the 1980s, Europe was ravaged by a series of seemingly senseless terrorist attacks on civilian targets.

On August 2nd, 1980, a bomb exploded at the Central Train Station in Bologna, Italy, killing 85 people and wounding more than 200. Since a series of bombings and attacks had been blamed on leftist extremists, many Italians were surprised when Prime Minister Francesco Cossiga and the authorities pinned the blame on an extreme-right group, Nuclei Armati Rivoluzionari (NAR). They were even more surprised when evidence implicated members of Italian military intelligence. A decade later, after Prime Minister Giulio Andreotti confirmed the existence of a secret army code-named Gladio, the surprise and shock deepened as accumulated evidence suggesting that US military intelligence and its NATO proxies were behind the terrorist campaign that had brutalized Cold War era Europe.[204]

What was the purpose of this apparently random violence? Swiss history professor Daniele Ganser writes:

> The terrorists, supplied by the (NATO-run) secret army, carried out bomb attacks in public places, blamed them on the Italian left, and were thereafter protected from prosecution by the military secret service. "You had to attack civilians, the people, women, children, innocent people, unknown people far removed from any political game," right-wing terrorist Vincezo Vinciguerra explained the so-called strategy of tension to Casson. "The reason was quite simple. They were supposed to force these people, the Italian public, to turn to the state to ask for greater security. This is the political logic that lies behind all the massacres and the bombings which remain unpunished, because the state cannot convict itself or declare itself responsible for what happened."[205]

These U.S.-NATO terrorist attacks on European civilians may have occurred in Germany, France, Spain, Portugal, Holland, Luxemburg, Belgium, Denmark, Norway, Greece, and Turkey, as well as Italy, the home of Operation Gladio proper. Besides forcing the people to turn to the state for security, US-military-sponsored terrorism in Europe had the added advantage of demonizing the peaceful, democratic left. U.S. policymakers were terrified that European leftist parties might win an election and take power. So the bombings carried out by U.S.-NATO proxies were blamed on the left, which was then discredited and prevented from coming to power, where it might have threatened to undermine US control of Europe.

Besides the many bombings, Operation Gladio and its analogues in other European countries sometimes included assassinations and shootings. In the Brabant province of Belgium, 28 people were killed and more than 20 injured in a series of shootings carried out with extreme military precision between 1982 and 1985. The US Defense Intelligence Agency, working through the NATO secret army, has been implicated in the Brabant massacre.[206]

Gladio's bloodiest work was carried out in Turkey, where the military junta was more than happy to cooperate with US intelligence agencies in massacring civilians and assassinating potential dissidents. The total number of innocent people slaughtered by Gladio and related US military-intelligence attacks on European civilians has been estimated in the thousands or even tens of thousands, with the greatest number of murders occurring in Turkey.[207]

On November 22, 1990, the European Parliament passed a resolution condemning Gladio. The resolution demanded a full investigation and the complete dissolution of Gladio's secret armies. Unfortunately, no full official investigation has yet transpired, and there is no evidence that NATO's paramilitary terrorist network has yet been dissolved. The European Parliament resolution stated that "in certain Member States military secret services (or uncontrolled branches thereof) were involved in serious cases of terrorism and crime," and blamed "certain US military personnel at SHAPE and in NATO" for the operations of the false-flag terror network.[208]

How can Europe's Parliament have exposed such an outrageous program of state-sponsored false-flag terror, yet failed to obtain a full investigation, or even any assurance that Gladio has been terminated? Is the secret government behind the false-flag terror networks more powerful than the official, formal government? Or are most people simply unwilling to fully face facts when the facts are this outrageous?

Should the Mossad Change Its Motto to "By Way of Deception Thou Shalt Get Caught"?

The motto of the Israeli Mossad is: "By way of deception thou shalt do war."

Since it began colonizing Palestine in the late 19th and early 20th centuries, the Zionist movement has used deception as its prime weapon. Zionists deceived British leaders into thinking they, the Zionists, would accept Britain's offer of a Jewish national home in Africa—when in fact the Zionists were secretly committed to a Jewish state in Palestine, and only in Palestine. Later, they deceived the world into thinking they only wanted a modest "national homeland" in Palestine rather than a full-fledged state. They deceived the world into thinking that they certainly were not intending to displace any native Palestinians, when in fact they knew full well that their plan for a Jewish state would require the ethnic cleansing of Palestine. They deceived the world into thinking that their Arab enemies were the aggressors and terrorists, and they the innocent victims, when in fact Israel was built on systematic Zionist aggression, terrorism, and theft, from the King David Hotel bombing, to Deir Yassin and the other massacres of 1948, to the attack on Egypt in 1967, the slaughter at the Sabra and Shatila refugee camps, the 2009 massacre of more than 1,000 innocent civilians in Gaza, and countless other horrors. In short, the history of Israel is an ongoing exercise of systematic state terrorism against the Palestinian population and its allies.

The truth about Israel's history is gradually emerging, thanks in part to the efforts of Israel's "new historians," who have shown that previous Palestinian accounts of such disputed events as the 1948 ethnic cleansing were true, while the standard Zionist narrative, parroted for decades in the Western media, was false.[209]

One aspect of Israeli history remains surrounded by numerous questions: Just how much false-flag terrorism have Zionists in general, and Mossad agents in particular, committed?

The Lavon Affair: Fifty Years of Israeli Lies?

The first well-known act of Israeli false-flag terrorism was the Lavon affair of 1954, during which Mossad agents infiltrated Egypt and planted bombs in American and British owned buildings, leaving telltale clues that would incriminate Arabs. The Mossad team even bombed a United States diplomatic facility! Unfortunately for the bombers, one of the bombs went off prematurely, and Egyptian police dragnet quickly rounded up the Mossad spies, one of whom may have been secretly working for the Egyptians. Despite the overwhelming evidence against them, the Israeli government falsely asserted its innocence and claimed the whole thing was an anti-Semitic hoax. Egypt responded with a public trial of the culprits, and proof emerged that bombings were part of an Israeli false-flag operation called Operation Susannah. Its purpose was to turn the U.K. and U.S.A. against the Egyptians.[210]

The Israeli government continued to lie outrageously for decades until finally, in March 2005, President Moshe Katzav officially admitted Israeli responsibility for the bombings, and lavished honors on nine of the false-flag state-sponsored terrorists.[211]

Was the Sinking of the U.S.S. Liberty Another Botched False-Flag Operation?

The Israeli government has admitted that the Lavon bombings were part of a botched Israeli false-flag terror operation. So far, it has not delivered a similar confession with regard to the murderous Israeli attack on the unarmed U.S. spy ship the U.S.S. Liberty on June 8, 1967. Perhaps Israel's slaughter of 34 defenseless sailors, and its wounding and maiming of more than 170 others, was simply too heinous a crime to admit.[212]

The U.S.S. Liberty was on a reconnaissance mission in international waters off the coast of the Sinai in the midst of the 1967 war between Israel and Egypt, flying a huge, easily visible U.S. flag, when it was viciously attacked by Israeli jet fighters and torpedo boats. The jet fighters made repeated passes, strafing the ship and even lifeboats full of survivors, while the torpedo boats attempted to finish the ship off and send it to the bottom. Though the initial attack had targeted the *Liberty*'s communications antenna, by patching together what was left of its communications equipment, the *Liberty* crew was miraculously able to send an S.O.S. message identifying the attackers as Israeli, forcing the Zionists to call off their butchery. Israel later claimed they had mistaken the U.S.S. *Liberty* for an Egyptian horse transport, the El Quseir, an ancient and decrepit vessel less than one-fourth the *Liberty*'s size. But the *Liberty*, a spanking-new high-tech ship bristling with antennae, could not have been mistaken for anything by the Israeli planes that approached to within fifty feet of the gigantic US flag. The *Liberty* survivors all know the attack was obviously intentional. But they were threatened, intimidated, and silenced for decades by higher-ups.

Why would Israel attack an American ship? Some argue the *Liberty* was in a position to spy on Israel's mass executions of Egyptian prisoners of war, a gross violation of the Geneva Conventions and a crime against humanity. Others have suggested that Israel was afraid that information gathered by the *Liberty* might somehow be used by Egypt.

The most plausible and thoroughly-documented hypothesis, however, is that the *Liberty* incident was a false-flag attack. According to Peter Hounem's *Operation Cyanide*, the sinking of the *Liberty* was intended to be blamed on Egypt, which would have given the Johnson Administration an excuse to enter the war on the side of Israel.[213]

Hounem uncovers evidence that the 1967 war was planned well in advance by American and Israeli hard-liners. The Israeli objective was to seize territory, while the American goal was to push back the Russians, who were winning widespread support in the Arab world with their backing of the popular Nasser regime in Egypt.

After invading Egypt with the connivance of the Johnson Administration, Israel lied to the world, inventing a false story about a nonexistent Egyptian attack. As Ambassador Michael Haddow put it as early as June 5th in a telegram to the Foreign Office, "It looks like the Israelis started it. We have been led up the garden path..."[214] The Zionist lies worked. "By the time the world caught on that there had been no Egyptian attack, the war was effectively won and the press were hailing Israel's brilliant success."[215]

According to Hounem's thesis, the *Liberty* was supposed to be sunk by Israel, and the attack blamed on Egypt, as an excuse for an all-out U.S. attack on Nasser and his Russian backers. He provides evidence that American nuclear-armed bombers were launched with orders to drop nuclear bombs on Russian military installations in Egypt, and that the planes were recalled less than two minutes before they would have been out of radio range. By keeping their ship afloat, and getting a message out about who their attackers really were, the heroic *Liberty* survivors may have prevented global thermonuclear war.

The Anthrax Attacks: A Still-Unsolved Hate Crime Against Muslims?

"Death to America. Death to Israel. Allah is great." Such was the message that accompanied the anthrax letters that followed the 9/11 attacks.[216]

Whoever sent the anthrax letters wanted Americans to think that Muslims had done it.

The Islamophobic motive of the attacks is the elephant in the living room. The anthrax criminals wanted to make Americans hate Muslims. And they wanted to convince Americans that Muslims who detest Israel also detest America.

After years of blaming Steven Hatfill, Bush's Justice Department seized on the apparent suicide of another Fort Detrick biowarfare scientist, Dr. Bruce Ivins, to claim that Ivins did it all by himself. Yet they admit that Ivins passed two lie detector tests.[217] They admit it wasn't his handwriting on the envelopes.[218] They admit that according to their own timeline, he couldn't have mailed the letters.[219] And they have not shown that he had a motive for perpetrating such a horrific hate crime against Muslims.

A 2009 study by Joseph Michael, a scientist at the Sandia National Laboratories in Albuquerque, New Mexico, found that the terror anthrax "doesn't match bacteria from a flask linked to Bruce Ivins."[220]

Why are they framing Dr. Bruce Ivins, who is dead and cannot defend himself? Is it because when they tried to frame a guy who was alive and kicking, Steven Hatfill, the scapegoat fought back and cleared his name?

And who are they covering for? Who might have had a motive for perpetrating an Islamophobic hate crime? And what kind of criminal is so important that the Justice Department orders the FBI to cover for him?

Are they covering for the Fort Detrick germ warfare scientist who was fired before 9/11 for racist harassment of a Muslim Egyptian co-worker? That scientist was caught sneaking back into the lab after hours, after he had been fired and had no right to be there.[221]

An anthrax criminal tried to frame that same Muslim Egyptian co-worker for the anthrax attacks. How do we know that? The letter fingering the co-worker was mailed before the anthrax attacks were public knowledge.[222]

But would the Justice Department really go to all the trouble of framing Steven Hatfill, then Bruce Ivins, just to cover for some crazy Islamophobe at Fort Detrick? Or was Bush's Justice Department hiding something truly sinister?

Former White House Policy Analyst Barbara Honegger informs us:

> Battelle Memorial Institute, a bio-defense contractor located in West Jefferson, Ohio, has exclusive control of the Ames strain contained in the mailed anthrax letters and, in partnership with the CIA and Defense Intelligence Agency, ran Project Jefferson, the government's covert and illegal offensive bio-weapons program whose goal was to develop a hyper-weaponized form of the anthrax Ames strain found in the letters... Battelle...also directs the anthrax experimentation at the U.S. military's Dugway Proving Ground in Utah, the second 'home' in addition to Ft. Detrick of the Ames strain contained in the anthrax letters.[223]

According to Honegger, Donald Rumsfeld announced on September 10th, 2001 that Operation Jefferson had succeeded in producing hyperweaponized anthrax.[224]

The anthrax attacks targeted Tom Daschle and Patrick Leahy, the two biggest roadblocks in the path of the Patriot Act.[225] The anthrax attacks were used by the Bush Administration as an excuse to shut down the FBI investigation of 9/11. The anthrax attacks convinced the American people that they had suffered a WMD attack by radical Muslims, and that horrific attacks from Muslims could be expected on a regular basis. Ultimately, the anthrax attacks helped convince the American people to murder more than a million Muslims in Iraq and Afghanistan.

By successively blaming Steven Hatfill and Bruce Ivins, both non-Muslims, the FBI has admitted that the anthrax attacks were a false-flag attack designed to falsely implicate Muslims. This despicable hate crime cries out for a real investigation.

9/11: Why So Many Unanswered Questions?

"Three thousand people are dead! Let's ask some real questions!" (9/11 family member to the 9/11 Commission before he was hauled out by security.)[226]

Jesse Ventura put it bluntly: "Why aren't we supposed to ask questions about 9/11?"

The 9/11 victims' family members have been emotionally devastated by the government's refusal to answer their questions. The Family Members' Steering Committee presented an extensive list of questions to the 9/11 Commission, which was charged with answering those and all other questions about the most important historical event of the 20th century.[227] Of those questions, the vast majority were left unanswered.

The 9/11 Commission's excuse for not answering the Family Members' questions was that it didn't have the resources to explore them. Indeed, the investigation, which the Bush Administration had frantically tried to prevent from occurring, got an initial appropriation of only three million dollars to investigate the biggest crime in history.[228] Compare that to the nearly 60 million dollars spent on the investigation of Bill Clinton's one act of consensual sex with Monica Lewinsky.[229]

Stop and think about that for a moment. 9/11 was a huge, sprawling mass murder—the crime of the century, with earth-shaking historical consequences. Clinton's "crime" was one sex act. Should not the 9/11 investigation have gotten thousands of times the funding of the Clinton sex investigation? Why wasn't the 9/11 investigation adequately funded? Who decided to keep it so small and weak? Was this investigation really meant to answer the unanswered questions? Or was it just a PR exercise?

When asked why so few of the skeptics' questions had been answered, Philip Zelikow, the main author of the *9/11 Commission Report*, said: "When we wrote the report, we were also careful not to answer all the theories. It's like playing Whack-A-Mole. You're never going to whack them all. . . ."[230]

Today, the co-chairs of the 9/11 Commission, Thomas Keane and Lee Hamilton, admit that the Commission was a failure, and that that was the plan all along: "So there were all kinds of reasons we thought we were set up to fail."[231]

During the long, dark night of the Bush Administration, those who questioned 9/11 rarely got answers, or even a reasonable hearing. Instead, they were insulted as "conspiracy theorists" and thereafter ignored. But now that America has elected a new president, the momentum is shifting. Today, hundreds of former high-level military, intelligence and administration officials, as well as scientists, engineers, architects, pilots, scholars, firefighters, lawyers, political leaders, medical professionals, and others with professional expertise are on the record expressing their skepticism about the official account of 9/11.[232] See www.patriotsquestion911.com for a stunning list of names and quotes. Among those questioning 9/11 can be found such highly-respected figures as General Wesley Clark, former Supreme Allied Commander Europe; Thomas Kean, Lee Hamilton, and six other members of the 9/11 Commission; Robert Baer, the former top CIA agent in the Middle East; Col. Robert Bowman, the Cal Tech rocket science Ph.D. who headed the U.S. space weapons program under Presidents Ford and Carter; the CIA's former presidents' daily briefer, Ray McGovern; Gore Vidal, the historical writer who is widely considered America's greatest political essayist; and many similarly illustrious individuals.

The recent explosion of 9/11 skepticism owes its existence to the many dedicated researchers who have investigated the questions that the Commission failed to answer. The most skillful and accomplished generalist scholar of 9/11 is Dr. David Ray Griffin, professor emeritus of philosophy and theology at Clairemont College of California. As of this writing Dr. Griffin has authored seven books on 9/11, beginning with *The New Pearl Harbor: Disturbing Questions About the Bush Administration and 9/11* (2004) whose chapter titles ask nine key questions about 9/11. Griffin's follow-up work *9/11 Contradictions: An Open Letter to Congress and the Press* (2008) is structured around a series of twenty-five questions about some of the glaring internal contradictions in the official story. My selection of what I consider the most glaring unanswered questions about 9/11 is indebted to the work of Dr. Griffin and other researchers.[233]

Was the Official Report a Cover-Up?

The Bush Administration frantically resisted proposals for an official investigation of 9/11 for more than 400 days. By comparison, it took about a week to set up investigations of previous disasters including Pearl Harbor, the Challenger disaster, and the JFK assassination.

According to 9/11 Commission co-chair Thomas Keane, the Commission was "set up to fail." Former FBI Director Louis Freeh has called the *Report* a cover-up.[234] Gen. Wesley Clark, former head of the U.S. European Command, says "We've never finished the investigation of 9/11 and whether the administration actually misused the intelligence information it had."[235] The Former Chief Weapons Inspector for Iraq, Maj. Scott Ritter says "I, like the others, are frustrated by the 9/11 Commission Report, by the lack of transparency on the part of the United States government, both in terms of the executive branch and the legislative branch when it comes to putting out on the table all facts known to the 9/11 case."[236] Robert Baer, the former top CIA agent in the Middle East, says "more than anything what we need right now is complete and total transparency on 9/11."[237] When asked about whether 9/11 might be an inside job, Baer responded "There is that possibility, the evidence points at it."[238] Former 9/11 Commssion counsel John Farmer states that the public has been "seriously misled about what occurred during the morning of the attacks" and that "at some level of the government, at some point in time…there was an agreement not to tell the truth about what happened."[239]

Indeed, there is general agreement among informed people that the *9/11 Commission Report* was a cover-up (it is impossible to find a serious defense of the *Report* in print). Yet none of the *Report*'s critics have elucidated its failings with the clarity, thoroughness and critical acumen that David Griffin applies in his magisterial *The 9/11 Commission Report: Omissions and Distortions*. In that book, Griffin calls the *Report* "a 571-page lie" and details more than 100 lies told by the Commission.[240]

Among the many lies told by the *9/11 Commission Report*, a few real whoppers stand out. One is the *Report*'s claim that the question of who paid for the 9/11 attacks is "of little practical significance."[241] Another is its description of the cores of the World Trade Center towers as hollow shafts, when in fact they consisted of the 47 massive core columns that held up each building.[242] (Those columns would have survived a pancake collapse or any other natural event; their destruction can only be explained by controlled demolition using explosives to slice through the columns.) A third monumental lie is the Commission's claim that Dick Cheney did not arrive in the Presidential Command Bunker until after 10 a.m., when witnesses including terror czar Richard Clarke have him there by around 9:15.

The Commission blames Osama Bin Laden and 19 young Arabs for the 9/11 attacks, yet presents not a shred of admissible evidence against any of them, while omitting volumes of exculpatory evidence.[243] Virtually all its claims about the alleged hijacking plot are based on supposed confessions allegedly extracted under torture from Khalid Sheikh Mohammed (KSM), yet the Commission had no access to KSM or even to recordings of any of his alleged confessions! Instead, the Commissioners had to rely on reports from KSM's torturers—war criminals whose word would not hold up in any court in the world.

In short, the real question is not whether there has been a 9/11 cover-up. Instead, it is: What are they covering up, and why?

How Much Foreknowledge Was There?

According to Bush's National Security Advisor Condoleeza Rice, nobody could have predicted that hijacked airplanes could be used as missiles. [244] Other White House officials and military spokespeople have made similar claims.[245]

That planes could serve as missiles is hardly difficult to imagine. Tom Clancy's 1994 bestseller *Debt of Honor* describes a passenger airliner deliberately crashing into the US Capitol.[246] And the March, 2001 pilot episode of *The Lone Gunmen* showed a 747

what about Odigo? Commander of the Secret service?

being flown into the World Trade Center by remote control, as part of a government conspiracy to trigger war.[247]

More importantly, a series of U.S. military studies, exercises and drills from 1993 through 2000 envisaged exactly this possibility—planes being used as missiles to attack national monuments, including the Pentagon and the World Trade Center.[248] That this was not a merely theoretical possibility is shown by the fact that in 1994 alone, three planes were actually hijacked with the intent to use them as missiles. One of the targets was the Eiffel Tower.[249]

So much for "nobody could have predicted." But what about actual specific foreknowledge of 9/11? FBI Director Robert Mueller said in 2002, "To this day we have found no-one in the United States except the actual hijackers who knew of the plot." Mueller must not have been looking very hard. Evidence of widespread specific foreknowledge of 9/11 in intelligence and financial circles, beyond the Israeli foreknowledge discussed below, is so abundant that it will be difficult to summarize briefly.

Perhaps the best-known example is the apparent insider trading that preceded 9/11.[250] Investors made huge sums of money betting on a stock price crash for American Airlines, United Airlines, and Morgan Stanley (a major tenant in the Twin Towers). Since these investments were made just days before 9/11, the investors apparently knew which airlines were going to hit which buildings when. The 9/11 Commission said not to worry, because the party that made the bets had "no conceivable ties to al-Qaeda."[251] Besides, the Commission added, it didn't really matter who financed the attacks: "To date, the U.S. government has not been able to determine the origin of the money used for the 9/11 attacks. Ultimately the question is of little practical significance."[252] In all other murder investigations, whoever pays for a murder is considered the author of the crime. Why then did the 9/11 Commission state that it considered the question of who was responsible for 9/11 to be "of little practical significance"?

Another example of specific foreknowledge has been provided by former FBI informant Randy Glass, who learned ahead of time that the Twin Towers were slated for destruction and tried to warn Florida Senator Bob Graham as well as his FBI superiors.[253] Rebuffed by Graham, Glass was referred by FBI colleagues to the

90

private phone number of high-ranking State Department Counter-Terror official Francis X. Taylor. Glass called Taylor and said "Listen, I already know about the World Trade Center." At that time, Glass did not know that the attack would involve airplanes. But his bluff elicited the following remark from Taylor: "*Randy, listen, you cannot mention any of these things, especially airplanes being used to fly into the World Trade Center.*" Taylor explained that the planes-into-WTC plot had to remain secret for geo-strategic reasons, and added: "Look, Randy, we know you're a straight guy, so we're going to give you some information. You cannot do two things: You cannot go to the media under any circumstances. This is—we're playing in a nuclear minefield now. Secondly, you can't tell the agents that you're working with now because they're out of the loop. They know nothing."[254]

Randy Glass is not the only FBI asset to have gained specific foreknowledge of 9/11. David Schippers, the high-ranking Republican who led the prosecution of Bill Clinton's impeachment, was contacted by FBI agents six weeks before 9/11. According to Schippers, those agents knew the date and targets of the upcoming 9/11 attacks and wanted to take action to prevent them, but had been silenced by threats from FBI superiors.[255] Schippers' account was confirmed by several FBI agents, according to *The New American* magazine.[256]

Why did the 9/11 Commission ignore these and many other instances of apparent foreknowledge? Why hasn't any of this information become the focus of a criminal investigation?

Why Didn't Bin Laden, or Any Other Radical Muslim, Take Credit for 9/11?

The stated goal of Osama Bin Laden and al-Qaeda is to force the US empire out of the Middle East and liberate Palestine from Zionist occupation. Bin Laden made public statements approving of the attack on the U.S.S. Cole and the bombings of U.S. embassies in Kenya and Tanzania. He has been indicted by the FBI for those crimes. Apparently, from Bin Laden's perspective, attacks on US military and diplomatic facilities abroad promise to weaken U.S. resolve and hasten the U.S.-Zionist departure from the occupied holy lands of Islam.

But could a massive passenger-jetliner attack on iconic civilian skyscrapers in the U.S. homeland—a spectacularly telegenic horror set-piece causing thousands of casualties—be expected to *weaken* U.S. resolve? Hardly. On the contrary, such an attack would be expected to cause U.S. policy to become even more imperialist, aggressive, and pro-Zionist. That is why no anti-imperialist Muslim, least of all Bin Laden, would be likely to orchestrate such a spectacular attack, unless he were spectacularly stupid. And anyone stupid enough to desire such an attack would clearly be far too stupid to successfully carry it out, unless they had a lot of help.

In any case, if Bin Laden or some other anti-imperialist Muslim really *were* that stupid, and still somehow managed to pull off such an attack, they would immediately take credit for their spectacular handiwork. But as we have seen, shortly after 9/11 Bin Laden clearly stated that he had nothing to do with the attacks: "I would like to assure the world that I did not plan the recent attacks, which seems to have been planned by people for personal reasons."[257] He even deplored the attacks as un-Islamic crimes against civilians: "I had no knowledge of these attacks, nor do I consider the killing of innocent women, children and other humans as an appreciable act."[258] The FBI apparently still thinks he was telling the truth, stating that Bin Laden is "not wanted" for 9/11 because there is "no hard evidence" against him.[259]

So if Bin Laden and his accomplices were really behind 9/11, why all the denials?

Is the So-Called Bin Laden Confession Video "Bogus"?

In December 2001, the media reported that an al-Qaeda home video had been discovered by some unnamed U.S. serviceman in a house in Jalalabad.[260] The extremely low-quality video was widely broadcast and touted as proof that despite his public denials, Bin Laden had at least privately confessed to involvement in—or at least foreknowledge of—the 9/11 attacks.

Skeptics immediately raised questions about the video. Did al-Qaeda really make home videos? If so, why would an organization skilled enough to defeat America's defenses on 911, and to make slick broadcast-quality videos on other occasions, produce such an incredibly bad video, whose production values were far worse than the average home video produced in an American trailer park?

And where did this video really come from? If it was in fact discovered in an empty house in Jalalabad by a U.S. serviceman, who precisely *was* this serviceman, and why was he not all over the media as the national hero who had proved Bin Laden's guilt? In short, if this video was supposed to be evidence of something, where was the chain of possession?

The questions didn't stop there. Why was the translation distorted to make Bin Laden's guilt clearer than the actual Arabic words would suggest? And why did the Osama in this video fail to resemble the Osama in other videos? Had he gained fifty pounds and gotten a nose job while hiding in his cave? Was the real Osama left-handed, and if so, why was this guy writing with his right hand? And wasn't Osama a jewelry-spurning fundamentalist? So why was he sporting a fancy ring? (Later, in 2007, a completely different-looking Osama who has apparently dyed his beard black, which no Islamic extremist would ever do, was again touted as authentic by the mainstream U.S. media.)

Professor Bruce Lawrence of Duke University is one of America's leading Bin Laden experts. When I asked him about this video, he paused, took a deep breath, and said: "It's bogus." Lawrence added that he has many acquaintances in the Homeland Security sector whose work focuses on Bin Laden, and they too all know that the "confession video" is bogus.

But wait a minute...if the "confession video" is bogus, then whoever produced it must have wanted to frame Bin Laden for 9/11. Why would anyone want to do that? Let's look in more detail at what Bruce Lawrence said on my radio show.

Me: "The trouble with that tape, of course, is that it seems to be false, or phony. The guy who's supposed to be Bin Laden looks like he weighs at least fifty pounds more than Osama, he has a totally different facial structure in some of the shots at least. What do you think of this 'smoking gun Fatty Bin Laden confession tape' as some people call it?"

Bruce Lawrence: "It's bogus. And I don't think I'm alone. I have, believe it or not, some friends in the United States government whom I talk (to) and (with) whom I listen, and I said to them, really? is this for real? that is passed on, and there are demurals, and I...I can't specify exactly who these people are, but they're some people who work on the 24/7 Bin Laden clock in various departments of Homeland Security, and they also know it's bogus. Then I said, well, why hasn't there been an open disavowal? And they said, well, because, you know, in some quarters, it really is convenient to say this guy did it all. And did it all that way. So, you know, the problem is, that...I don't want to say this government only excels in, or practices, disinformation. But on the question of 9/11, and Bin Laden's role in it, there is as you correctly said, Kevin, a kind of master narrative that really begins with the premise that he must have done it. Because if one tears open just a little bit that slick covering of public misinformation, and says 'who would have done it if not Bin Laden,' it's pretty horrific." (You can hear the exchange at www.radiodujour.com/people/lawrence_bruce/.)

Was America Really Attacked by Muslims?

The *9/11 Commission Report* blames Islamic "extremism" and "fundamentalism" for the worst catastrophe in U.S. history. Specifically, it blames the "extreme Islamist version of history" and "what for want of a better term is often labeled 'fundamentalism.'"[261] Due to their extremist fundamentalism, the 9/11 Commission informs us, the 19 alleged hijackers were "fanatically" religious and formed a "cadre of trained operatives willing to die."[262] Yet overwhelming evidence shows that the 19 men accused of sacrificing their lives in an act of fanatical extremist fundamentalism were neither fanatics nor extremists nor fundamentalists. In fact, they were not even practicing Muslims.

According to the *Wall Street Journal*, several of the alleged hijackers were heavy drinkers who were regular customers of porn shops and strip clubs.[263] According to the *San Francisco Chronicle*, Atta and other hijackers "engaged in some decidedly un-Islamic sampling of prohibited pleasures" during their many trips to Las Vegas.[264] The mayor of Patterson, New Jersey, confirmed that the alleged hijackers there were utterly un-religious: "Nobody ever saw them at mosques, but they liked the go-go clubs."[265] On September 10th, 2001, three of the alleged hijackers spent a total of about $750 on lap dances and alcohol in a Florida sex club.[266] Afterwards, two of them spend over $1000 on strippers and champagne in another bar.[267]

It is completely unthinkable that any practicing Muslim—much less a fanatical extremist fundamentalist about to sacrifice his life in hopes of gaining paradise—would behave this way. So if these 19 individuals were involved in the attacks, it would be not just inaccurate, but an actual blood libel, to claim that America was attacked by Muslims on September 11th, 2001.

For a more detailed critical examination of whether any Muslims were involved in 9/11, see David Ray Griffin's essay "Was America Attacked by Muslims on 9/11?"[268]

Where Were the Fighter Jets?[269]

At 8:14 a.m. on September 11th, 2001, American Airlines Flight 11 failed to respond to an FAA ground control order, and its transponder and radio went off. By 8:21 it was known to have veered off-course. Normally, when these signs of an in-flight emergency occur, the FAA controllers quickly try to reestablish contact and, if unsuccessful, immediately notify NORAD, which scrambles fighter jets to intercept the errant plane. This procedure is *always* followed when a plane is off-course, since that presents a threat to other planes.[270] Since fighter jets with top speeds of over 1800 miles per hour are stationed throughout the US and are always on alert, they normally intercept errant planes within ten minutes of the original detection of the in-flight emergency. Such interceptions are standard procedure, and happen roughly 100 times per year. The usual result is for the fighter jet to rock its wings as a signal to "follow me," then guide the errant plane to its proper course.[271]

Why wasn't Flight 11 intercepted?

If standard operating procedure had been followed on 9/11, Flight 11 would have been intercepted, and probably shot down, before it reached New York.[272] For some reason this did not happen. Instead, Flight 11, unmolested by America's air defenses, hit the North Tower at 8:46 a.m.

Why wasn't Flight 175 intercepted?

Meanwhile, at 8:42, United Airlines Flight 175 lost its radio and transponder signal and went off-course. At this point the FAA and the military knew that Flight 11 had been hijacked and was heading into New York City. The FAA, following standard operating procedure, notified NORAD at 8:43. Griffin writes: "NORAD should have had fighter jets intercepting this plane by 8:53. And by this time, being 7 minutes after the first hijacked plane had hit the WTC, the fighters certainly should have been ready to shoot down this second hijacked plane if it did not immediately follow orders."[273]

But once again, America's air defenses went AWOL. With no fighter jets in sight, Flight 175 hit the South Tower at 9:03. The military has told several conflicting stories about why they failed.[274] According to the latest story (as of this writing) the US military claims it never even knew there was a problem with Flight 175 until after it hit the South Tower. The FAA, of course, maintains that it did its job, and notified the military at 8:46. Other sources say the military closely monitors domestic air traffic, and would have known about Flight 175's problems even without being told by the FAA.[275]

How could Flight 77 hit the Pentagon, without any reaction from U.S. air defenses, almost 90 minutes after the FAA knew that planes were shutting off their transponders and veering wildly off-course, and almost an hour after the first Tower was struck?

American Airlines Flight 11 first went off-course at 8:46, lost radio contact at 8:50, and lost its transponder signal at 8:56. Still, no fighter jets were launched, even though all of this happened shortly after the North Tower had been struck. At 9:37, fifty-one minutes after it had first gone off course, Flight 11 (according to the official story) flew through America's most heavily-guarded airspace unmolested, and slammed into the Pentagon, the best-defended building in the best-defended city on the planet.[276] Though an E4-B "flying Pentagon" command and control aircraft was lazily circling over the White House before and after the Pentagon was hit, no fighter jets were in sight. Today, the military is still lying as it continues to deny the presence of the E4-B, despite abundant video and photo evidence and even mainstream media reports proving the E4-B was there. What was it doing there, and why is the military still lying about it?[277]

United Airlines Flight 93 was believed hijacked, according to FAA personnel and the FBI, by around 9:30. The FBI was allegedly monitoring alleged cell phone calls from passengers—which were physically impossible, given 2001 cell phone technology[278]—before 9:45. Yet according to the latest version of the official story, Flight 93 crashed near Shanksville, Pennsylvania at 10:03 without US air defenses even knowing about any problems with the flight. In fact, the U.S. military (in its latest of three contradictory stories explaining why it went AWOL on 9/11) claims that the FAA never even notified it about the problems with flights 175, 11, and 93 until after each of those planes, respectively, had crashed![279] FAA personnel beg to disagree. They say the military was notified in a timely manner in all four cases.[280] (Additional evidence suggests that the military must have known about all four in-flight emergencies right away, even without notification from the FAA.)[281]

Why did the world's most sophisticated air defense system do nothing for almost two hours while the nation was under attack from the air on September 11th, 2001—when on other days, even relatively minor in-flight emergencies result in interception by fighter jets within minutes? Why did the U.S. military offer three successive contradictory, increasingly unbelievable stories purporting to explain why it went AWOL on 9/11? Why has the military and the 9/11 Commission (in the latest official story) indirectly accused FAA personnel of the grossest and most unbelievable forms of criminal negligence, yet nobody from the FAA has even been reprimanded, much less fired or prosecuted? What explains the contradiction between the military's and 9/11 Commission's horrific accusations against the FAA, and the assertions by FAA personnel that they followed standard operating procedure in a timely manner? Why have the co-chairs of the 9/11 Commission, Thomas Kean and Lee Hamilton, accused the military of lying, and said they considered referring top U.S. military officials for perjury prosecutions?[282] Why, given the outrageous contradictions between the two official stories top military personnel gave to the 9/11 Commission, have these prosecutions not yet transpired?[283]

Why Did the Secret Service Keep Bush in the Florida Classroom?[284]

Everyone who has seen Michael Moore's *Farenheit 9/11* knows that after Bush was notified at 9:04 a.m. that America was under attack, he just stared into space with a guilty look on his face as the children in Booker Elementary School read *My Pet Goat*. This bizarre performance continued for an excruciating eight or nine minutes. Then Bush praised the students' reading skills, chatted with the children, posed for photos, and gave a brief televised address at 9:29, exactly as planned in his pre-announced schedule. Bush and his Secret Service entourage exited the school in a leisurely manner, and the presidential limousine took the pre-announced route to the airport. During the trip to the airport, Bush and the Secret Service got word of the Pentagon strike. Yet no fighter jet escort was ordered for Air Force One, which unhurriedly took off at around 9:55.

Secret Service protocols dictate that if there is any suspicion that the nation might be under attack, the President is whisked away to safely immediately. The President, after all, is at the top of the chain of command. He has the codes for the "nuclear football," the briefcase that follows the President everywhere he goes and that would allow him to give the command to launch nuclear weapons. Any attack on America, it is assumed, would target the President in an attempt to decapitate the chain of command.

At 9:04 a.m. on September 11th, everyone, including Bush and the Secret Service, knew the USA was under attack from the air. Yet for almost an hour, the President dawdled in pre-announced locations, while thousands of potentially hijacked airliners remained in the skies. Why didn't the Secret Service follow its own protocols and whisk the President to safety? What could possibly explain this gross dereliction of duty? Did the commander of the Secret Service team in Florida know that the President was not a target? How could he have known this?

What Happened to Building 7 and the Twin Towers?

(Note: Much of the following material needs to be seen to be fully appreciated. An excellent resource is Richard Gage's video

Blueprint for Truth, *available at* www.ae911truth.org, *which supports the following analysis.*)

World Trade Center Building 7 was a 47-story skyscraper that would have qualified as the tallest building in most American states, and one of the most robust buildings in the world. Built over a power substation, Building 7 had unusually massive steel frame members. It was never hit by a plane, and there is no evidence that it suffered from any serious fires. Photographs show only a few small fires in a few windows, chiefly on 7th and 12th floors. Yet at 5:20 p.m. on September 11th, 2001, World Trade Center Building 7 collapsed straight down into its own footprint in six-and-one-half seconds—roughly the same speed that an object would fall through thin air.[285]

Prior to September 11th, 2001, no tall building on earth had ever completely collapsed for any reason except controlled demolition. As David Griffin has pointed out, the collapses of Building 7 and the Twin Towers exhibited eleven *exclusive* features of controlled demolition.[286] That means that not one of these eleven phenomena have ever happened to any building, anywhere, except during controlled demolitions. Let's go ahead and ask the hard questions about these exclusive characteristics of controlled demolition that also characterized the three alleged fire-induced collapses on 9/11.

What caused the sudden onset of collapse?

In controlled demolitions, explosives blow away the building's vertical supports all at once. Observers watch a perfectly motionless building suddenly begin to collapse when all vertical support is removed. Fire, or any other natural cause, cannot suddenly slice all of a building's steel frame members at the same time. Thus a fire-induced collapse, if such a thing were possible, would begin gradually, as the steel warped, buckled, and sagged asymmetrically.

The onset of the collapse of Building 7 (and the Towers) was very sudden. Videotapes show that WTC-7's roofline is completely immobile at one moment, then begins to move downward all at once in the next moment. This always happens with controlled demolitions, and has never happened anywhere outside of controlled demolitions...except, allegedly, three times in the same city on the same day: NYC, September 11th, 2001.

Why did the three buildings fall straight down?

Any natural collapse of skyscraper, whether from fire, earthquake, tornado, poor construction, or any other cause, should be asymmetrical. In plain English, the building will topple. Why? Because no natural process can remove all the vertical support holding up different parts of the building at the same time. Controlled demolition companies have to work very hard to ensure that their explosives cut all vertical support simultaneously at each level, to bring buildings straight down instead of toppling them onto neighboring buildings. They also have to make sure the charges on each of the targeted floors go off with absolute precision.To understand how hard this is, think of a lumberjack charged with bringing a giant redwood straight down onto its stump. The sudden loss of vertical support at any one part of the tree would cause the part above to topple, while the part below would remain standing. To get the whole thing to come straight down, the tree would need to be sliced through very quickly in many places. That's what controlled demolition experts do with buildings. It is extremely difficult to engineer this kind of vertical collapse, which is why controlled demolition companies charge millions of dollars for their services. How could relatively small office fires have the same effect? Yet the only official explanation for WTC-7's collapse, the years-overdue NIST report of August 2008, blames office fires alone—dismissing prior speculation that diesel fuel in a basement tank, or structural damage, played a role.

Building 7, like the Twin Towers, came straight down. Danny Jowenko, one of Europe's top demolition experts, was unfamiliar with alternative theories about 9/11. When Jowenko was shown the video of the collapse of Building 7, he expressed certainty that it was a controlled demolition, and complete befuddlement about how this could have happened on 9/11.[287]

How could the three buildings come down at free-fall speed?

Building 7 came down in 6.5 seconds. That is the same speed that objects fall through thin air. According to experts like Richard Gage, an architect who has designed steel-frame buildings, any collapse from natural causes could not possibly occur at free-fall speed. For a building to come down at free-fall speed, all of the building's vertical support must suddenly disappear. No natural cause can remove all vertical support with the perfect timing required to achieve a vertical free-fall collapse, according to Gage and other experts. Why are hundreds of architects and engineers risking their careers to state this publicly?[288]

Why did the three buildings suffer complete collapse?

All previous collapses of apartment buildings and other tall, vertical structures have been partial, asymmetrical collapses, leaving much of the building relatively intact. This is because only some vertical support gets removed, not all vertical support, leaving much of the structure intact, while only a portion of it fails. Yet Building 7 (and the Twin Towers) collapsed completely. No tall building before or since 9/11 has ever completely collapsed for any reason but controlled demolition. Were there really three exceptions, all in the same city on the same day? Doesn't that stretch the laws of probability just a wee bit?

What sliced the steel?

In order for all vertical support in a tall building to suddenly disappear, the steel columns must be sliced. Some extremely high-temperature process, presumably involving explosives, sliced the steel columns of Building 7 (and the Twin Towers). The *New York Times* reported that portions of the structural steel from Building 7 had not only been melted, but actually evaporated![289] Though virtually all of the structural steel from Building 7 and the Towers was quickly removed and disposed of before it could be properly investigated, photographic evidence exists showing the same kind of diagonal column cuts that are typically made by demolition charges. How could these diagonal slices with once-molten edges conceivably result from any kind of natural collapse?

What pulverized the concrete, office equipment, furnishings, and people into dust clouds?

The destruction of Building 7 (and the Twin Towers) produced huge, roiling dust clouds reminiscent of controlled demolitions. There is no evidence that any such dust clouds have never been produced by any natural building collapse. Why not? Because without the energy provided by explosives, the concrete might shatter into small pieces, but there is no mechanism that could turn it to ultra-fine dust and hurl it outward in roiling, rapidly-expanding clouds. Only the energy provided by explosives can do that. Explosives pulverize concrete and other materials, and blast the dust outward with the force necessary to produce the kind of roiling clouds we all saw on 9/11. Computer engineer Jim Hoffman has calculated that it would have required far more energy than that available from gravity alone to produce the amount of dust resulting from the demise of the Twin Towers and turn it into rapidly-expanding dust clouds.[290]

Hoffman also points out that dust clouds were produced during the first few seconds of collapse, when the relative motion of the top and bottom sections was just a few feet per second. And engineer Jeff King notes that dust clouds were created far above the impact zone.[291] What mechanism could have produced these dust clouds?

Had the Towers collapsed due to gravity, as the official theory holds, the result would have been a pile of jagged pieces of concrete more than ten stories high. Inside that pile of concrete, there would have been office equipment, furniture, and human bodies, crushed but still more or less intact. The body of every person killed in the collapse would have been found, and almost all of them would have been relatively intact.

But in reality, the destruction of the Towers left a tiny pile of rubble that was a few stories high in some places, and ground-level in others. Rescue workers pointed out that this tiny "pile" contained no desks, no chairs, no computers, no telephones, and very few intact human bodies. Everything had been pulverized. Of the roughly 2,500 people killed in the Towers, only a little over half have been identified from their remains. In most cases, these people were identified from tiny bodily fragments, not intact bodies. More than 1000 people presumed killed in the Towers have never been so identified. That means that not a single fragment of any of those bodies has ever been found. Like most of the concrete, office furnishings and equipment, these human beings were somehow turned to the fine powder and shards that roiled outward in pyroclastic clouds and produced a "snowfall" several inches deep throughout most of Manhattan.

102

Six years after 9/11, tiny bone fragments of 9/11 victims were found on top of the Deutche Bank building across the street. What reduced these human skeletons to one-centimeter shards and blasted them across the street? Can gravity cause human beings to explode into tiny fragments and accelerate sideways hundreds of feet through the air?

Does the crimp in the roofline indicate that the core columns were pulled first?

Controlled demolitions begin by slicing the core columns in the center of the building, causing the outer walls to be pulled inward. The purpose is to make sure the building comes down into its own footprint, rather than toppling sideways and damaging neighboring structures.

As Alex Jones has pointed out, the fall of Building 7 begins when the roofline sags in the center—what Jones calls "a classic crimp." Were the central supports of Building 7 taken out first, so the walls would fall inward into the building's footprint?

Likewise, the fall of the North Tower was preceded by a crimp that caused the antenna on its rooftop to begin moving downward just before the collapse began. The antenna was in the middle of the rooftop, an area supported by the central core columns. Evidently those columns were severed a split second before the others, as happens in controlled demolitions. There is no evidence that central columns have suddenly given way, a split second before general collapse, in any building that collapsed by natural causes before or after 9/11. This phenomenon is another exclusive hallmark of controlled demolition. You can witness it firsthand by googling "North Tower antenna drop" and "WTC -7" and watching videos of these events. After watching the videos, what do you think caused the crimp in Building 7's roofline and the North Tower antenna drop?

What caused the demolition rings and "squibs" ?

Relatively small explosions that spiral around a building in rapid-fire sequence are a common characteristic of controlled demolitions. So are "squibs"—horizontal puffs of dust blasted outward by explosives. Both of these phenomena were produced in the collapses of Building 7 and the Twin Towers. Neither has ever been witnessed anywhere in history except during controlled demolitions...and, allegedly, during three supposedly natural, fire-induced skyscraper collapses on 9/11. What caused these phenomena?

Why were there so many sounds of explosions?

According to witness testimonials and audio recordings, there were numerous explosions in the Twin Towers, beginning before the planes hit, and in Building 7, beginning at shortly after 9 a.m. As in a Fourth of July fireworks display, the explosions in the Twin Towers continued sporadically until the massive eruption of explosions in the "grand finale" that brought the Towers down. Never in history has any building collapse been preceded by such explosions, except in cases of controlled demolition. How could three allegedly fire-induced collapses have all produced the sound of explosions in such abundance?

What melted the steel?

Molten steel was found beneath the rubble of Building 7 and the Twin Towers. What produced it? Fire produced by jet fuel and office furnishings cannot burn nearly hot enough to significantly weaken structural steel, much less melt it. In fact, the maximum theoretical temperature for an open-air hydrocarbon fire, under perfect laboratory conditions, is roughly 1000 degrees Fahrenheit less than the temperature required to melt steel. No steel has ever been melted, in all history, by any high-rise fire or natural building collapse.

The kinds of explosives used in controlled demolitions do melt steel, as they cut through it like a hot knife through butter. Given all of the other evidence, isn't this a good, simple, straightforward explanation of how so much steel came to be melted?

What caused the horizontal ejections?

In addition to these ten exclusive characteristics of controlled demolition, all of which apply to both Building 7 and the Twin Towers, there is another anomalous phenomenon that occurred during the destruction of the Towers: horizontal ejections.

It wasn't just dust that exploded sideways out of the Towers. Along with the dust, huge chunks of aluminum cladding were blasted more than 700 feet outward, and multi-ton pieces of steel were flung more than 500 feet in a horizontal trajectory to impale themselves in neighboring buildings.

Never before in any gravity-driven building collapse—or any gravity-driven event of any kind—have heavy objects "fallen" by accelerating horizontally at tremendous speeds. Was the law of gravity suspended on 9/11/01?

Why have the government's many conflicting explanations of what happened to these buildings been so inadequate?

As Kevin Ryan points out, the same core group of people, including some who ran the very questionable Oklahoma City bombing investigation, were responsible for most of the official "explanations" of what happened to the three skyscrapers on 9/11.[292] Oddly, all of these official explanations conflict with each other. And none of them adequately address any of the points raised above.

The first explanation we heard on 9/11 itself, from physical scientists who obviously knew better, was that fire from the jet fuel and office furnishings had melted the steel.[293] Why did these scientists invent such a preposterous lie? As we have seen, such fires cannot possibly come within ever one thousand degrees of melting steel. Could these scientists possibly have been that stupid?

The next explanation came from a team hired by Larry Silverstein, who we will meet again in a later section. The Silverstein-Weidlinger investigation's column-failure theory would be quickly repudiated by everyone, but it was good enough for Silverstein to walk away with more than 4 billion dollars in cash profits from his six-week investment in the asbestos-ridden, money-losing Twin Towers.[294]

Then came the FEMA report on the collapse of the Towers, echoed by a NOVA TV special, blaming a floor-by-floor pancake collapse.[295] There were three obvious problems with this theory. First, where were the pancakes? If each floor had slammed into the floor below it, dislodging it from its vertical supports and causing it in turn to crash into the next floor below, we would have seen a fifteen-story-tall pile of 110 floors stacked up like pancakes, with squashed humans, computers, desks, chairs, telephones, and so on in between the floors. But there was no such pile at Ground Zero. Instead, there was just some chopped steel and aluminum, a little bit of concrete, and a whole lot of dust, most of which settled far away from the site. Most of the concrete, furniture, office equipment, and human beings had been pulverized into dust and shards and blasted all over Manhattan, leaving only a tiny pile at Ground Zero that varied from ground level to a couple of floors high.

The second problem with FEMA's pancake theory was that a pancake collapse, if such a thing were possible, would take place over a minute or so. It could not happen at freefall speed. Why not? Because each floor's fall would be slowed as it crashed into the floor below.

The third problem with the pancake theory was that while it purported to explain how the floors could fall, it could not explain what happened to the 47 massive steel core columns. In a real pancake collapse (again, assuming such a thing were possible) these 47 columns would have been left intact, jutting skyward out of the pile of pancakes like a record-player spindle towering above a fallen stack of lp records.

These three obvious defects condemned FEMA and NOVA's pancake theory to a quick demise, at least among those who were paying attention. Unfortunately, many Americans watched the NOVA special and had this obviously false explanation engraved in their memory.

The next government body charged with explaining the demise of the three skyscrapers was the 9/11 Commission itself. Unfortunately, the 9/11 Commission made no attempt at a scientific explanation of what happened to the Towers. It even lied by claiming that the cores of the Towers were hollow, when in fact they contained the 47 massive steel core columns that held each building up. Worse, the *9/11 Commission Report* never once mentioned the destruction of Building 7.[296]

Then along came the National Institute of Standards and Technology (NIST) with what it claimed was the final report on the Towers, and, years later, a long-overdue report on Building 7. Both reports admitted that the earlier pancake theory was false, and both blamed fire for the collapses.

NIST's 10,000-page report on the Towers admits that it cannot explain the collapses. Why not? Presumably because there is absolutely no way that any natural process could cause sudden, vertical, symmetrical, free-fall speed collapses. Instead, NIST spends 10,000 pages explaining what it calls "collapse initiation," not the collapse itself—which NIST seems to be implicitly admitting is impossible to explain without invoking controlled demolition. And even its purported explanation of collapse initation "is now known to be false in every aspect."[297]

What exactly is "collapse initiation"? According to NIST, it is the fire-induced loss of vertical support on a few floors in the plane strike zone. Once that vertical support was lost, NIST claims, the intact top section of the building came crashing down on the intact bottom section of the building like a jackhammer. How this could then produce a complete, vertical, free-fall collapse NIST does not even attempt to explain.

Two years after NIST's 10,000-page non-explanation of the destruction of the Towers, the same agency put out its years-overdue report on Building 7. It was the first-ever official explanation of what happened to Building 7, and it was even more unsatisfactory than the report on the Towers. Dismissing absurd claims that damage from the falling Towers or diesel fuel in the basement caused the demise of Building 7, NIST once again blamed ordinary office fires for what appears to be a classic controlled demolition. Yet vastly worse fires have raged in other high-rises, without even weakening the steel, much less causing any kind of collapse, least of all a sudden, complete, vertical, free-fall collapse! The NIST report on Building 7 was so inadequate that even Dr. Frank Greening, the only independent scientist who has ever seriously attempted to defend the various government accounts of what happened to the World Trade Center, called it a work of fiction.[298]

In April 2009, nine scientists published a paper entitled "Active Thermitic Material Discovered in Dust from the 9/11 World Trade Center Catastrophe."[299] The study, published in a mainstream peer-reviewed chemical engineering journal, "shows that dust from the collapsing towers contained a 'nano-thermite' material that is highly explosive." One of the authors, physicist Steven Jones, said there is no benign explanation for the presence of nano-thermite, a high-tech explosive material developed in the years prior to 9/11 at government military labs.[300] The paper appears to present absolute proof of controlled demolition.

When will we get a real investigation to address the unanswered questions about the destruction of the World Trade Center?

Obviously we need a genuine investigation of the catastrophic loss of these three skyscrapers. Such an investigation should have subpoena power, and should be led by skeptics including members of Architects and Engineers for 9/11 Truth, Scholars for 9/11 Truth and Justice, SPINE, and other professional associations that have questioned the earlier, inadequate accounts.

Why Was World Trade Center Owner Larry Silverstein Never Investigated for Arson?

David Ray Griffin writes: "It certainly seems beyond belief that Silverstein, who had made almost $500 million in profit from the collapse of Building 7, would reveal not only that the building was deliberately demolished but that he himself had made the recommendation."[301]

Beyond belief or not, Larry Silverstein is on the record saying of Building 7 that on 9/11 he suggested "maybe the smartest thing to do is pull it" and then "they made that decision to pull, and we watched the building collapse."[302] "Pull" is an industry term for controlled demolition.[303]

Silverstein, who had owned Building 7 since it was built, took over the rest of the World Trade Center on July 24th, 2001—six weeks before the destruction of the entire complex.[304] The previous owner, the New York Port Authority, had carried a grand total of 1.5 billion dollars of insurance for all of the buildings.[305] Silverstein demanded, and got, 3.5 billion worth of insurance, payable in cash if the WTC were to be destroyed.[306] Shortly after putting up only 14 million dollars of his own money for the deal, "Lucky Larry" Silverstein just happened to skip a very important meeting in the WTC on 9/11 because, he claims, his wife insisted that he visit his dermatologist.[307] Likewise two of his children, who should have been at the Windows on the World restaurant atop the North Tower (where they would have died) miraculously survived because they just happened to be running late that day.[308]

After 9/11, Silverstein demanded double indemnity, claiming that the two plane crashes constituted separate terrorist attacks.[309] He soon walked away with more than 4.5 billion dollars cash from his 3.5 billion dollar insurance policy.[310] But apparently that four-billion-dollar profit on his six-week investment wasn't enough. On March 27th, 2008, the *New York Times* reported that Silverstein was back in court asking for another 12.3 billion dollars from airlines and airport security companies.[311]

Silverstein's prospective 17-billion-dollar payoff on a 14-million-dollar down payment might qualify as the world's best-ever investment. But had 9/11 not occurred, Silverstein's purchase of the World Trade Center could have qualified as the world's *worst*-ever investment. According to Trade Center plans, 5,000 tons of asbestos were going to be used in the Twin Towers,[312] much of that total was actually used, and estimates of the amount that remained in the Towers on 9/11 range from 400 to 2000 tons.[313] On May 14th, 2001, *Business Insurance* magazine reported that the Port Authority had just lost a $600 million asbestos abatement lawsuit against its insurers.[314] Given that the Twin Towers were reputed to be money-hemorrhaging white elephants plagued not just with asbestos, but also with low vacancy rates due to their lacking any modern communications infrastructure, and that the Port Authority had reportedly been trying to find a way to demolish them but was prevented from doing so by the asbestos problem,[315] Larry Silverstein's decision to take out a 99-year-lease on the World Trade Center makes very little sense unless he somehow knew they were slated for quick extra-legal demolition.

When someone buys a dubious, asbestos-ridden property, doubles the insurance policy, and sees the property destroyed by fire and/or explosives six weeks later, an arson investigation normally follows. If the person of interest were to publicly confess to participating in the intentional destruction of said property, one would expect not only an investigation, but also a swift indictment, prosecution, and conviction.

Why hasn't Larry Silverstein even been investigated?

Was Israel Involved?

"Lucky Larry" Silverstein just happens to be a close personal friend of Benyamin Netanyahu, the radical Zionist Israeli leader who invented the War on Terror back in 1979, and who is on record publicly celebrating the 9/11 attacks.

Other circumstantial evidence for Israeli involvement in 9/11—or at least foreknowledge—includes:

• Reports in the Bergen, New Jersey *Record* of September 12, 2001 that five Israelis were arrested in New York on 9/11 "carrying maps linking them to the blasts."[316] The article stated that Israelis in an Urban Moving Systems van were also arrested after they were caught filming and wildly celebrating the destruction of the Twin Towers. ABC-TV's *20-20* later stated that the driver of the van, Sylvan Kurzberg, told police: "We are Israelis. We are not your problem. Your problems are our problems. The Palestinians are your problem."[317] ABC reported that one of the Israelis was carrying two foreign passports, while another had $4,700 cash stuffed in his sock.[318] Not surprisingly, "the FBI believed Urban Moving may have been providing cover for an Israeli intelligence operation."[319] Held for 71 days, the four men—Paul Kurzberg, Yaron Shmuel, Oded Ellner and Omer Marmari were deported to Israel. One of them later stated on an Israeli talk show: "Our purpose was to document the event."[320] But how had they known there would be an event to document?

• Carl Cameron's four-part investigative series on Fox News documenting a massive Israeli intelligence operation against the U.S. during the six months leading up to 9/11. According to Cameron, a highly-placed FBI source said "evidence linking these Israelis to 9/11 is classified. I cannot tell you about the evidence that has been gathered. It's classified information."[321] Senate Intelligence Committee Chair Bob Graham (D-FL) echoed the suggestion about "classified information": "I think there is very compelling evidence that at least some of the terrorists were assisted not just in financing—although that was part of it—by a sovereign foreign government ... It will become public at some point when it's turned over to the archives, but that's 20 or 30 years from now."[322] (What "sovereign foreign government" has an American lobby powerful enough to keep such information classified for 20 or 30 years?) The French newpaper *Le Monde* added details in a report headlined "An Enigma: Vast Israeli Spy Network Dismantled in the US."[323] *Salon.com* reported that some of the Israeli spies were "living down the street from Mohammed Atta's house."[324] *Salon* Journalist Christopher Ketcham was told by a high-level U.S. intelligence source: "The problem is that you're going into a hornet's nest with this. It's a very difficult time in this particular area. This is a scenario where a lot of people are living a bunker mentality....There are a lot of people under a lot of pressure right now because there's a great effort to discredit the story, discredit the connections, prevent people from going any further [in investigating the matter]. There are some very, very smart people who have taken a lot of heat on this—have gone to what I would consider extraordinary risks to reach out. Quite frankly, there are a lot of patriots out there who'd like to remain alive. Typically, patriots are dead."[325]

• Reports in the Israeli newspaper Haaretz that "that two workers at the Israeli company Odigo Instant Messaging Systems "received messages two hours before the Twin Towers attack on September 11 predicting the attack would happen."[326]

• Reports that Zim Israeli-American Shipping Lines vacated its World Trade Center offices, breaking its lease to do so, one week before 9/11.[327] These reports of Israeli foreknowledge may explain why so few Israelis died in the Twin Towers, in proportion to Israel's presence in New York financial circles, compared to citizens of other nations.

• Reports that the Israeli company ITCS handled security at Boston's Logan Airport, where flights 11 and 175 took off, as well as "every other airport where planes were hijacked on 9/11."[328]

Speaking of the wide-scale Israeli intelligence operation in the US prior to and on 9/11, University of Minnesota peace studies professor Michael Andregg says of the Isreali spies, "They were here—and lots of them. The question is, why?"[329] In his video *Rethinking 9/11*, Andregg urgently pleads with the Israeli Prime Minister to reveal the truth about this operation to the American people.

What Happened to the Pentagon Videos?

We all saw the images of planes hitting the Twin Towers. On and shortly after 9/11, the media broadcast those images so many times that if anyone had wanted to watch something else on television, they would have had to move to a far-off land, or maybe even a distant planet.

We are also told that another horrific, spectacular attack happened that day. We are told that terrorists seized control of a Boeing 757 and crashed it into the Pentagon in Washington, D.C., the planet's most important military headquarters. We are told that this crash caused a fire so hot that it vaporized the aluminum from the plane. We are told...and told...and told...but we have never actually *seen* the attack on the Pentagon. Why not?

Academy Award winning filmmaker Michael Moore said: "I've filmed there before down at the Pentagon—before 9/11—there's got to be at least 100 cameras, ringing that building, in the trees, everywhere. They've got that plane coming in with 100 angles. How come we haven't seen the straight—I'm not talking about stop-action photos, I'm talking about the video. I want to see the video; I want to see 100 videos that exist of this."[330] In 2006, after the Pentagon finally released one poor-quality tape that purports to show the attack on the Pentagon, but does not show any airliner, CNN's Jamie McIntyre reported that "there are at least 80 other tapes that the government is holding onto" including some that show the attack aircraft.[331]

Why would the U.S. government refuse to show its 80 (or 100) surveillance videos of the attack on the Pentagon? One would think one or more of those videos would have been all over the news on 9/11, alongside the WTC crash images.

Much of the world does not believe that any commercial airliner hit the Pentagon. In March, 2002, Thierry Meyssan published a book arguing that a missile, not Flight 77, hit the Pentagon.[332] The British newspaper *The Guardian* described Meyssan as "president of the Voltaire Network, a respected independent think tank whose left-leaning research projects have until now been the considered models of reasonableness and objectivity."[333] Meyssan's book, *L'Effroyable Imposture* ("The Hideous Fraud") was an instant bestseller. Its powerful effect on public opinion helped turn France, as well as most of Europe and the Arab and Muslim worlds, against Bush's plans to invade Iraq. When Meyssan faced off against a spokesperson for the Pentagon on al-Jazeera TV, the Arab world's flagship network, a running poll showed that over 80% of the audience agreed with Meyssan that 9/11 was perpetrated by elements of the American government, not by al-Qaeda.[334]

Had the Bush Administration wanted to prove Meyssan wrong, and gain a huge advantage in its struggle to convince world public opinion to support its war plans, all it had to do was release the videos of the Pentagon hit...assuming, that is, that the videos show an American Airlines 757 hitting the Pentagon.

It isn't just Pentagon security videos that the government is withholding. Just minutes after the attack on the Pentagon, FBI officials showed up at the Citgo gas station across the street and confiscated the station's security videos showing the attack. (How could they have arrived so quickly?) A few minutes later, the FBI confiscated security videos from the Sheraton Hotel also showing the Pentagon attack. Neither video has ever been released, despite Freedom of Information Act lawsuits by the right-wing group Judicial Watch that specifically demanded those two videos.[335] In 2006, the Pentagon released one low-quality security video that appeared to show the vapor trail of a missile hitting the Pentagon. (Planes do not leave vapor trails at ground level, yet the video in question appears to show a vapor trail being left by an object, clearly smaller than a 757, caught in its final split-seconds before hitting the Pentagon.) For unknown reasons Judicial Watch did not protest the government's refusal to release the two confiscated videos and other Pentagon attack videos, nor did it ask why the released Pentagon video is dated 9/12/01 and appears to show a missile vapor trail being left by an object much smaller than a 757.

Could Hani Hanjour Have Flow Flight 77's Alleged Trajectory? And Why Would Any Terrorist Have Wanted To?

Alleged Flight 77 terrorist Hani Hanjour was just about the world's worst pilot, according to flight school instructors who refused to let him solo in a Cessna training aircraft. "He could not fly at all," one said. Yet according to the Bush Administration's official version of 9/11, Hanjour took the controls of a Boeing 757 over Ohio at more than 30,000 feet of elevation, turned it around, made a beeline for Washington, D.C., and for unknown reasons performed an incredible stunt maneuver in order to hit the newly-reinforced, relatively empty West Wing of the Pentagon—the part of the building furthest away from Donald Rumsfeld and the rest of the top brass. Had he simply plunged directly into the top of the building, instead of circling around it in a steep banking dive and stunt-flying in at ground level, Hanjour (or any terrorist) could have killed thousands, including top brass.

Hanjour finished his amazing flight, according to the Bush Administration story, by plunging through an 8,000-foot steeply-banking dive in two minutes, leveling off to skim the ground and clip light poles before managing to hit only the first floor of the Pentagon without leaving so much as a scratch on the lawn, which remained putting-green perfect right up to the small "757 hole" in the first floor.

The questions about Hanjour's alleged stunt-flight are legion. Why would such an important mission be entrusted to a dufus who couldn't even fly a Cessna? Why didn't America's air defense forces intercept Hanjour long before he allegedly hit the building at 9:37—almost an hour after the North Tower had been struck? Why does the alleged Flight 77 black box data provided by the U.S. government show a trajectory that takes the plane over the building, not into it?[336] And why is that trajectory, which agrees with most confirmed eyewitness accounts, different from the government's alleged trajectory in many other ways?[337]

Why is there so much evidence suggesting that most or all of the damage was done by bombs, rather than by a plane crash and/or missile strike? Why is there so little evidence of plane wreckage? What happened to the 100 tons of metal that supposedly crashed into the building? Does the government really expect us to believe that 100 tons of aluminum was vaporized by an open-air hydrocarbon fire? Why does eyewitness and victim April Gallop, a Pentagon worker who walked out the hole in the building carrying her baby, report that there was no wreckage or any other evidence of a plane crash? Gallop reports that she has spoken with many other witnesses, and that none of them saw any evidence of a plane crash at the Pentagon.[338]

Other questions center on the time of the attack on the Pentagon. If it happened at 9:37, as the Bush Administration said, why do eyewitnesses and stopped clocks agree that the attack came at 9:31?[339]

And what was a "flying Pentagon" E4-B ultra-advanced command and control aircraft doing circling over Washington D.C. around the time of the Pentagon attack?

What Really Happened at the "Crash Site" in Shanksville, Pennsylvania—and at the Other Alleged Crash Sites?

If Flight 93 really crashed in Shanksville, why was there so little evidence of a crash at the alleged crash site? Photos show a fifteen-foot-diameter hole in the ground and not much else. What happened to the plane?

Consider the following transcript from Fox News on 9/11/01:

FOX News reporter: I wanna get quickly to Chris Chaniki he's a photographer with the Pittsburgh affiliate a Fox affiliate. He was back there just a couple minutes ago and Chris, I've seen the pictures, it looks like there's nothing there, except for a hole in the ground.

Chaniki: Basically that's right, the only thing you can see from; where we were was a big gouge in the earth, and some broken trees. You could see some people working, walking around in the area, but from where we can see there wasn't much left.

Reporter: Any large pieces of debris at all?

Chaniki: No, there was nothing. Nothing, that you can distinguish that a plane had crashed there.

Reporter: Smoke, fire?

Chaniki: Nothing, it was absolutely quiet, it was actually very quiet. Nothing going on down there, no smoke, no fire, just a couple of people walking around. They look like part of the NTSB crew. Walking around, looking at the pieces.

Reporter: How big would you say that hole was?

Chaniki: Ah, from my estimates, I would guess it was probably around 20 to 15 feet, ah long, and probably about 10 feet wide.

Reporter: What could you see on the ground, if anything, other than dirt and ash and ... ?

Chaniki: You couldn't see anything. You just see dirt, ash and people walking around, broken trees.

According to U.S. Air Force Col. George Nelson (ret.) not one piece of identifiable debris has been produced from any of the four alleged crash sites on 9/11.[340] Col. Nelson explains that this is astonishing, since airliners are constructed of parts that have serial numbers and dates, so they can be replaced at the proper time. It is therefore a simple matter to identify a plane based on its parts. Yet on 9/11, the FBI appears to have prevented the National Transportation Safety Board (NTSB) from conducting a standard forensic investigation of the alleged crash sites. Why?

More questions surround the alleged recovery of Flight 77's black box at the Pentagon, and the alleged non-recovery of the black boxes of Flights 11 and 175 at the World Trade Center. Regarding Flight 77, the government has released its alleged black box data, but that data records a plane following a completely different path from the one that supposedly knocked down lightpoles and put a hole in the first floor of the Pentagon.[341] In fact, the government's own black box data appears to record a plane flying *over* the Pentagon, not crashing into it.[342] Additionally, the story about when this black box was recovered is highly implausible, due to contradictions in its timeline.[343]

In contrast to the magically-appearing black box at the Pentagon, consider the magically-disappearing black boxes at the World Trade Center. Two New York City firefighters, Mike Bellone and Nicholas De Masi, have reported accompanying government agents during their recovery of the black boxes from the World Trade Center debris.[344] Yet the government's official position is that the black boxes of Flights 11 and 175 were never recovered. What happened to the black boxes the workers saw? How could an alleged hijacker's passport survive the inferno and float to earth miraculously unscathed—while the black boxes, which are designed to be utterly indestructible, were somehow vaporized?

116

Dave Lindorff asks: "Why would the main intelligence and law enforcement arm of the U.S. government (the FBI) want to hide from the public not just the available information about the two hijacked flights that provided the motivation and justification for the nation's 'War on Terror' and for its two wars against Afghanistan and Iraq, but even the fact that it has the devices which could contain that information?"[345]

Afterword: "The Truth Will Set You Free?"

When you are imprisoned by lies, it may seem that the truth will set you free. But what really sets you free may not be the truth itself, but the process of fearless questioning that leads toward it.

In short, it may be questions that set you free—not truth.

In Orwell's *1984*, Winston Smith learns the truth, but it does not set him free. The truth is that the world is ruled by an inner party that uses fear-mongering and lies to enslave the rest of the population. As he discovers this, Winston has the truth shoved down his throat as he is tortured back into the zombie-like complacency from which he had so briefly awakened.

What is missing from the world of *1984* is not so much truth as the habit of fearless questioning that, in healthier societies, topples idols and keeps liars on their toes. The population of Orwell's dystopia has been beaten down to the point that it is unable to question the information it is being fed by the authorities. In such a culture of complacency, the awakening of a few individuals to the truth has little effect. What is needed is the sudden outbreak of an epidemic of questioning.

The journey toward truth has no final destination in this world. Yet it does have a clear direction—out of the shadows and into the light. The milestones that mark this journey are the questions that disillusion us, that free us from the untruths we had mistaken for truths.

The master of the disillusioning question was, of course, Socrates.

If Socrates were alive today, he would be questioning the War on Terror.

One Final Question for the Reader: What do you think of these quotes about truth and falsehood?

Poetry is nearer to vital truth than history.
Plato

Every truth has two sides; it is as well to look at
both, before we commit ourselves to either.
Aesop

Something unpleasant is coming when
men are anxious to tell the truth.
Benjamin Disraeli

Great is truth, but still greater, from a practical point of
view, is silence about truth. By simply not mentioning
certain subjects... totalitarian propagandists have
influenced opinion much more effectively than they
could have by the most eloquent denunciations.
Aldous Huxley

If an eloquent speaker speak not the truth, is there
a more horrid kind of object in creation?
Thomas Carlyle

It is possible to be a master in false philosophy, easier, in fact,
than to be a master in the truth, because a false philosophy
can be made as simple and consistent as one pleases.

The dreamer can know no truth, not even about
his dream, except by awaking out of it.
George Santayana

People will generally accept facts as truth only if the
facts agree with what they already believe.
Andy Rooney

A harmful truth is better than a useful lie.
Thomas Mann

If you shut the door to all errors, truth will be shut out.
Rabindranath Tagore

And we should consider every day lost on which we have
not danced at least once. And we should call every truth
false which was not accompanied by at least one laugh.

There are various eyes. Even the Sphinx has eyes: and as a result there are various truths, and as a result there is no truth.

All things are subject to interpretation whichever interpretation prevails at a given time is a function of power and not truth.

Convictions are more dangerous foes of truth than lies.
Friedrich Nietzsche

What is truth? said jesting Pilate; and would not stay for an answer.
Francis Bacon

The victor will never be asked if he told the truth.
How fortunate for leaders that people do not think.
Adolf Hitler

It is the merit of a general to impart good news, and to conceal the truth.
Sophocles

A lie told often enough becomes truth.
Vladimir Lenin

The very concept of objective truth is fading out of the world. Lies will pass into history.

For a creative writer possession of the "truth" is less important than emotional sincerity.
George Orwell

Half a truth is often a great lie.
Benjamin Franklin

If you ever injected truth into politics you have no politics.
Will Rogers

A lie would have no sense unless the truth were felt as dangerous.
Alfred Adler

There are people who are very highly paid to cover the truth and who will protect their clients.
Mary Hart

Truth is on the side of the oppressed.
Malcolm X

[handwritten note: Amira Baraka ex poet laureate of New Jersey]

119

The "Way," without truth, is not life, but death.

Without truth, all "ways" lead to death. This is true
of every institution of faith, religious, political,
academic and commercial… even family.
David McIntosh

There are certain persons for whom pure Truth is a poison.
Andre Maurois

Truth forever on the scaffold, wrong forever on the throne.

Once to every person and nation come the moment to decide. In
the conflict of truth with falsehood, for the good or evil side.
James Russell Lowell

There is never vulgarity in a whole truth, however commonplace.
It may be unimportant or painful. It cannot be vulgar.
Vulgarity is only in concealment of truth, or in affectation.
John Ruskin

Exaggeration is truth that has lost its temper.

Many a doctrine is like a window pane. We see
truth through it but it divides us from truth.
Kahlil Gibran

Truth is so obscure in these times, and falsehood so established,
that, unless we love the truth, we cannot know it.
Blaise Pascal

All truth, in the long run, is only common sense clarified.
Thomas Huxley

Do I think I was put here on earth to be a
journalist and to seek truth? No, I don't.
Peter Jennings

The function of news is to signalize an event; the function of truth
is to bring to light the hidden facts, to set them in relation with
each other, and make a picture of reality on which men can act.

When distant and unfamiliar and complex things are
communicated to great masses of people, the truth
suffers a considerable and often a radical distortion. The

complex is made over into the simple, the hypothetical
into the dogmatic, and the relative into an absolute.
Walter Lippmann

The discovery of truth is prevented more effectively, not
by the false appearance things present and which mislead
into error, not directly by weakness of the reasoning
powers, but by preconceived opinion, by prejudice.
Arthur Schopenhauer

I always divide people into two groups. Those who
live by what they know to be a lie, and those who live
by what they believe, falsely, to be the truth.
Christopher Hampton

The truth is found when men are free to pursue it.
Franklin D. Roosevelt

Without free speech no search for truth is
possible... no discovery of truth is useful.
Charles Bradlaugh

Everyone wishes to have truth on his side, but not
everyone wishes to be on the side of truth.
Richard Whately

I wanted to write about the moment when your addictions
no longer hide the truth from you. When your whole
life breaks down. That's the moment when you have to
somehow choose what your life is going to be about.
Chuck Palahniuk

A truth that's told with bad intent
Beats all the Lies you can invent.
William Blake

An error is the more dangerous in proportion
to the degree of truth which it contains.
Henri Frederic Amiel

So near is falsehood to truth that a wise man would
do well not to trust himself on the narrow edge.

In everything truth surpasses the imitation and copy.

Marcus Tullius Cicero

Truth, like light, blinds. Falsehood, on the contrary, is
a beautiful twilight that enhances every object.
Albert Camus

The words of truth are always paradoxical.
Lao Tzu

Time is precious, but truth is more precious than time.
Benjamin Disraeli

Knowledge rests not upon truth alone, but upon error also.
Carl Jung

Adversity is the first path to truth.
Lord Byron

You shall know the truth, and the truth shall make you mad.
Aldous Huxley

The truth will set you free, but first it will make you miserable.
James A. Garfield

You know what the Englishman's idea of compromise is? He says,
Some people say there is a God. Some people say there is no God.
The truth probably lies somewhere between these two statements.
William Butler Yeats

Unless people can be kept in the dark, it is best for
those who love the truth to give them the full light.
Richard Whately

Any fool can tell the truth, but it requires a man
of some sense to know how to lie well.
Samuel Butler

If you do not tell the truth about yourself you
cannot tell it about other people.
Virginia Woolf

Truth lives, in fact, for the most part on a credit system. Our
thoughts and beliefs pass, so long as nothing challenges them,
just as bank-notes pass so long as nobody refuses them.

William James

Some counterfeits reproduce so very well the truth that it would be a flaw of judgment not to be deceived by them.
Francois de La Rochefoucauld

Truth is always served by great minds, even if they fight it.
Jean Rostand

The first reaction to truth is hatred.
Tertullian

There is little more powerful than when truth joins action.
Bryant H. McGill

The sad truth is that most evil is done by people who never make up their minds to be good or evil.
Hannah Arendt

In wartime, truth is so precious that she should always be attended by a bodyguard of lies.

We occasionally stumble over the truth, but most of us pick ourselves up and hurry off as if nothing had happened.
Winston Churchill

He who knows nothing is closer to the truth than he whose mind is filled with falsehoods and errors.
Thomas Jefferson

Man approaches the unattainable truth through a succession of errors.
Aldous Huxley

Never question the relevance of truth, but always question the truth of relevance.
Craig Bruce

No one can be happy who has been thrust outside the pale of truth. And there are two ways that one can be removed from this realm: by lying, or by being lied to.
Lucius Annaeus Seneca

Truth makes many appeals, not the least
of which is its power to shock.
Jules Renard

Even in literature and art, no man who bothers about
originality will ever be original: whereas if you simply
try to tell the truth (without caring twopence how often
it has been told before) you will, nine times out of ten,
become original without ever having noticed it.
C.S. Lewis

In a controversy the instant we feel anger we have already ceased
striving for the truth, and have begun striving for ourselves.
Buddha

As scarce as truth is, the supply has always
been in excess of the demand.
Josh Billings

An honest man speaks the truth, though it may give
offence; a vain man, in order that it may.
William Hazlitt

Everything will line up perfectly when knowing and living
the truth becomes more important than looking good.
Alan Cohen

It is one thing to show a man that he is in an error, and
another to put him in possession of the truth.
John Locke

Truth is the most valuable thing we have. Let us economize it.
Mark Twain

By and large, language is a tool for concealing the truth.
George Carlin

The truth is that parents are not really interested
in justice. They just want quiet.
Bill Cosby

Son, always tell the truth. Then you'll never have
to remember what you said the last time.
Sam Rayburn

Truth is like the sun. You can shut it out
for a time, but it ain't goin' away.
Elvis Presley

All the truth in the world adds up to one big lie.
Bob Dylan

We cripple ourselves with lies.
Jim Morrison

I've always had a problem with people who couldn't tell
the truth or admit a mistake and say they're wrong.
Burt Bacharach

A good man often appears gauche simply because he does
not take advantage of the myriad mean little chances of
making himself look stylish. Preferring truth to form, he is
not constantly at work upon the facade of his appearance.
Alanis Morissette

Truth can be stated in a thousand different
ways, yet each one can be true.
Swami Vivekananda

I speak the truth not so much as I would, but as much
as I dare, and I dare a little more as I grow older.
Michel de Montaigne

To tell the truth is revolutionary.
Antonio Gramsci

The only people I have seen who have been truly pushing
for the truth (about 9/11) are the family members.
Sibel Edmonds, US Government whistleblower

Always speak the truth, think before you
speak, and write it down afterwards.
Lewis Carroll

The truth is always something that is told, not something that is known. If there were no speaking or writing, there would be no truth about anything. There would only be what is.
Susan Sontag

There is no truth without responsibility following in its wake.
Kenneth L. Pike

Unless we provide consequences for activities and actions that are wrong, we are not going to get any truth.
Dana Rohrabacher

Truth has no special time of its own. Its hour is now—always.
One truth stands firm. All that happens in world history rests on something spiritual. If the spiritual is strong, it creates world history. If it is weak, it suffers world history.
Albert Schweitzer

In times of universal deceit, telling the truth becomes a revolutionary act.
George Orwell

Time discovers truth.
Lucius Annaeus Seneca

Humility is truth.
Desiderius Erasmus

No Flag Large enough
To Cover the Shame
of Killing Innocent Civilians
H. Zinn

I have been given the authority over you, and I am not the best of you. If I do well, help me; and if I do wrong, set me right. Sincere regard for truth.
Abu Bakr

The greatest friend of Truth is time, her greatest enemy is Prejudice, and her constant companion Humility.
Charles Caleb Colton

Time is the father of truth, its mother is our mind.
Giordano Bruno

Love is the father of truth, courage is its mother. Truth is born wherever the two are united.
David McIntosh

126

Yesterday we obeyed kings and bent our necks
before emperors. But today we kneel only to truth,
follow only beauty, and obey only love.

Of life's two chief prizes, beauty and truth, I found the first
in a loving heart and the second in a laborer's hand.

Truth is a deep kindness that teaches us to be content in our
everyday life and share with the people the same happiness.
Kahlil Gibran

The truth is lived, not taught.
Hermann Hesse

Doubt, indulged and cherished, is in danger of becoming
denial; but if honest, and bent on thorough investigation,
it may soon lead to full establishment of the truth.
Ambrose Bierce

To kill an error is as good a service as, and sometimes
even better than, the establishing of a new truth or fact.
Charles Darwin

If you are out to describe the truth, leave elegance to the tailor.
Albert Einstein

I believe that unarmed truth and unconditional
love will have the final word.
Martin Luther King, Jr.

Truth cannot be defeated.
Edwin Louis Cole

The truth is incontrovertible, malice may attack it,
ignorance may deride it, but in the end; there it is.
Winston Churchill

Justice is truth in action.
Benjamin Disraeli

Freedom and order are not incompatible... truth is
strength... free discussion is the very life of truth.

The more rapidly truth is spread among mankind the better
it will be for them. Only let us be sure that it is the truth.
Thomas Huxley

127

For my part, whatever anguish of spirit it may cost, I am willing to know the whole truth; to know the worst and provide for it.
Patrick Henry

There is not a truth existing which I fear... or would wish unknown to the whole world.

Truth is certainly a branch of morality and a very important one to society.
Thomas Jefferson

Truth will ultimately prevail where there is pains to bring it to light.
George Washington

It is a universal truth that the loss of liberty at home is to be charged to the provisions against danger, real or pretended, from abroad.
James Madison

I am a firm believer in the people. If given the truth, they can be depended upon to meet any national crisis. The great point is to bring them the real facts.
Abraham Lincoln

He who sees the truth, let him proclaim it, without asking who is for it or who is against it.
Henry George, American political economist

Clouds and darkness surround us, yet Heaven is just, and the day of triumph will surely come, when justice and truth will be vindicated.
Mary T. Lincoln

You will find that the truth is often unpopular and the contest between agreeable fancy and disagreeable fact is unequal. For, in the vernacular, we Americans are suckers for good news.
Adlai E. Stevenson

Intense feeling too often obscures the truth.
Harry S. Truman

We are not afraid to entrust the American people with unpleasant facts, foreign ideas, alien philosophies, and competitive values. A nation that is afraid to let its people judge the truth and falsehood in an open market is a nation that is afraid of its people.
John F. Kennedy

The great enemy of the truth is very often not the lie: deliberate, continued, and dishonest; but the myth: persistent, persuasive, and unrealistic.

The goal of education is the advancement of knowledge and the dissemination of truth.
John F. Kennedy

Let us begin by committing ourselves to the truth to see it like it is, and tell it like it is, to find the truth, to speak the truth, and to live the truth.
Richard M. Nixon

Richard Nixon is a no good, lying bastard. He can lie out of both sides of his mouth at the same time, and if he ever caught himself telling the truth, he'd lie just to keep his hand in.
Harry S. Truman

Tell the truth, work hard, and come to dinner on time.
Gerald R. Ford

If we are going to stay a great power and I hope and pray we will we need the truth. We need to know what is going right and we need to know what is going wrong. There is no greater time than now.
Charles Schumer, US Senator

In order that all men may be taught to speak the truth, it is necessary that all likewise should learn to hear it.
Samuel Johnson

When I can look life in the eyes, grown calm and very coldly wise, life will have given me the truth, and taken in exchange—my youth.
Sara Teasdale

It is good to express a thing twice right at the outset and so to give it a right foot and also a left one. Truth can surely stand on one leg, but with two it will be able to walk and get around.
Friedrich Nietzsche

Wisdom is found only in truth.
Johann Wolfgang von Goethe

If you look for truth, you may find comfort in the end; if you look for comfort you will not get either comfort or truth only soft soap and wishful thinking to begin, and in the end, despair.

Reason is the natural order of truth; but imagination is the organ of meaning.
C. S. Lewis

The profoundest of all sensualities is the sense of truth and the next deepest sensual experience is the sense of justice.
David Herbert Lawrence

The truth is merely a matter of fact whereas honesty is a question of attitude.
Tim Maher-DeTroyer

But the attitude of faith is to let go, and become open to truth, whatever it might turn out to be.
Alan Watts

Nothing gives rest but the sincere search for truth.

We know the truth, not only by the reason, but also by the heart.
Blaise Pascal

'Beauty is truth, truth beauty,'—that is all ye know on earth, and all ye need to know.
John Keats

I believe that it is better to tell the truth than a lie. I believe it is better to be free than to be a slave. And I believe it is better to know than to be ignorant.
H. L. Mencken

Opinions are made to be changed—or how is truth to be got at?
Lord Byron

To rise from error to truth is rare and beautiful.
Victor Hugo

For every good reason there is to lie, there
is a better reason to tell the truth.
Bo Bennett

Nothing in man is more serious than his sense of
humor; it is the sign that he wants all the truth.
Mark Van Doren

Piety requires us to honor truth above our friends.
Aristotle

To the living we owe respect, but to the dead we owe only the truth.
Voltaire

When a woman tells the truth she is creating the
possibility for more truth around her.
Adrienne Rich

Tell the children the truth.
Bob Marley

The pursuit of truth and beauty is a sphere of activity in
which we are permitted to remain children all our lives.
Albert Einstein

The very essence of a scientist's life is the service of truth.
Franz Boas

The truth is more important than the facts.
Frank Lloyd Wright

A lie can travel half way around the world
while the truth is putting on its shoes.

Truth is stranger than fiction, but it is because Fiction
is obliged to stick to possibilities; Truth isn't.
Mark Twain

There is nothing so strong or safe in an
emergency of life as the simple truth.
Charles Dickens

Rather than love, than money, than fame, give me truth.

It takes two to speak the truth: one to speak, and another to hear.

No face which we can give to a matter will stead us so
well at last as the truth. This alone wears well.
Henry David Thoreau

Truth is tough. It will not break, like a bubble, at
a touch; nay, you may kick it about all day like a
football, and it will be round and full at evening.
Oliver Wendell Holmes

There are also two kinds of truths: truth of reasoning
and truths of fact. Truths of reasoning are necessary
and their opposite is impossible; those of fact are
contingent and their opposite is possible.
Gottfried Leibniz

Metaphors have a way of holding the most truth in the least space.
Orson Scott Card

A remark generally hurts in proportion to its truth.
Will Rogers

What does it matter how one comes by the truth so
long as one pounces upon it and lives by it?
Henry Miller

Stand upright, speak thy thoughts, declare The truth
thou hast, that all may share; Be bold, proclaim
it everywhere: They only live who dare.
Voltaire

All truth passes through three stages. First, it is ridiculed. Second,
it is violently opposed. Third, it is accepted as being self-evident.
Arthur Schopenhauer

Nothing is more noble, nothing more venerable than
fidelity. Faithfulness and truth are the most sacred
excellences and endowments of the human mind.
Nature has planted in our minds an
insatiable longing to see the truth.
Marcus Tullius Cicero

Truth is the beginning of every good to the
gods, and of every good to man.
Plato

Plato is dear to me, but dearer still is truth.
Aristotle

Falsehood is easy, truth so difficult.
George Eliot

This is our lives. The way to give it dignity is to tell the truth.
Lee Grant

What we have in us of the image of God
is the love of truth and justice.
Demosthenes

Language is the house of the truth of Being.
Martin Heidegger

The best jihad is a word of truth flung in the face of a tyrant.
-The Prophet Muhammad, peace upon him

I am the Way, the Truth and the Life.
Jesus of Nazareth, peace upon him

Unless one always speaks the truth, one cannot
find God Who is the soul of truth.
Ramakrishna

When we believe ourselves in possession of the only truth,
we are likely to be indifferent to common everyday truths.
Eric Hoffer

The truth of our faith becomes a matter of ridicule
among the infidels if any Catholic, not gifted with
the necessary scientific learning, presents as dogma
what scientific scrutiny shows to be false.
Saint Thomas Aquinas

There are only two mistakes one can make along the
road to truth; not going all the way, and not starting.

Three things cannot be long hidden: the
sun, the moon, and the truth.

Teach this triple truth to all: A generous heart,
kind speech, and a life of service and compassion
are the things which renew humanity.
Buddha

Speak the truth, do not yield to anger, give, if thou art asked
for little; by these three steps thou wilt go near the gods.
Confucius

When virtue is lost, benevolence appears, when benevolence
is lost right conduct appears, when right conduct is lost,
expedience appears. Expediency is the mere shadow
of right and truth; it is the beginning of disorder.
Lao Tzu

An error does not become truth by reason of multiplied
propagation, nor does truth become error because nobody sees it.

Even if you are a minority of one, the truth is the truth

Truth stands, even if there be no public support. It is self-sustained.

Truth is by nature self-evident. As soon as you remove the
cobwebs of ignorance that surround it, it shines clear.

Truth and Non-violence are as old as the hills. All I have done
is to try experiments in both on as vast a scale as I could.

Morality is the basis of things and truth
is the substance of all morality.

My religion is based on truth and non-violence. Truth is
my God. Non-violence is the means of realising Him.

God, as Truth, has been for me a treasure beyond
price. May He be so to every one of us.

The pursuit of truth does not permit violence on one's opponent.

Truth never damages a cause that is just.

Violent means will give violent freedom. That would
be a menace to the world and to India herself.
Gandhi

The truth is cruel, but it can be loved, and it
makes free those who have loved it.
George Santayana

Truth is exact correspondence with reality.
Paramahansa Yogananda

The first step toward finding God, Who is Truth, is to discover the truth about myself: and if I have been in error, this first step to truth is the discovery of my error.
Thomas Merton

I value unity because I believe we learn truth from each other in this process.
Rowan Williams

It is one of the severest tests of friendship to tell your friend his faults. So to love a man that you cannot bear to see a stain upon him, and to speak painful truth through loving words, that is friendship.
Henry Ward Beecher

Friendship at first sight, like love at first sight, is said to be the only truth.
Herman Melville

Every scientific truth goes through three states: first, people say it conflicts with the Bible; next, they say it has been discovered before; lastly, they say they always believed it.
Louis Agassiz

Light is meaningful only in relation to darkness, and truth presupposes error. It is these mingled opposites which people our life, which make it pungent, intoxicating. We only exist in terms of this conflict, in the zone where black and white clash.
Louis Aragon

Two elements are needed to form a truth—a fact and an abstraction.
Remy de Gourmont

The thing you fear most has no power. Your fear of it is what has the power. Facing the truth really will set you free.
Oprah Winfrey

OK, so truth hurts—but what else does truth do?
Teena Marie

Truth is the property of no individual but is the treasure of all men.
Ralph Waldo Emerson

Tell the truth and shame the devil.
Francois Rabelais

The pursuit of truth will set you free; even
if you never catch up with it.
Clarence Darrow

Art is not a study of positive reality, it is the seeking for ideal truth.
John Ruskin

The theatre was created to tell people the truth
about life and the social situation.
Stella Adler

The well of true wit is truth itself.
George Meredith

A lot of truth is said in jest.
Eminem

My way of joking is to tell the truth. That's
the funniest joke in the world.
Muhammad Ali

I left in love, in laughter, and in truth, and wherever
truth, love and laughter abide, I am there in spirit.
Bill Hicks

sophia smallstorm

francisco cossiga

Richard Andrew Grove
Ellen Mariani
The Lockerbie holdouts

What We Can Do

"The ascendancy of Barack Obama to the presidency of the United States must be analyzed first and foremost not through its leadership, but through the base that brought this election to fruition. That base is fundamentally more progressive than its leadership. It is this organized base that is most capable of making the old adage true: 'If the people will lead, the leaders will follow.'" James Jordan, Co-Coordinator for the Respect for Democracy Campaign, March 1, 2009

The only way to get the change we voted for is to mobilize and make it happen.

Nothing will really change until the War on Terror is officially over—dead, buried, with a stake driven through its evil, lying heart. To do that, we need open, highly-publicized public hearings on Bush era war crimes and other crimes against humanity. Those crimes are of such a magnitude and nature that once nationally televised war crimes hearings begin, a groundswell of outrage will arise and do the rest. A page will turn, and the ugliest chapter in the history of American democracy—a chapter that was very nearly the final chapter—will be over. A new era, an age in which America can begin to live up to her potential as a light unto the nations, will begin.

Together, we can make it happen.

We can create a Bush Truth and Reconciliation Commission similar to the one that helped reveal and heal the crimes of the apartheid era in South Africa. Senator Patrick Leahy, who was attacked with U.S. government anthrax shortly after 9/11, has proposed such a Truth and Reconciliation Commission. We can all help realize this goal by going to www.BushTruthCommission.com and signing the petition, and then contacting our elected representatives to demand the establishment of a Bush Truth Commission as envisioned by Senator Leahy. Also check out www.democrats.com/special-prosecutor-for-bush-war-crimes.

We can force the government of New York City to establish a truly independent commission to carry out the first real investigation of the 9/11 attacks. Go to www.NYCcan.org to find out how.

We can support those who, like Native American activist Splitting-the-Sky, are committing civil resistance (CR) by attempting to perform citizens' arrests of Bush and other war criminals. Visit www.splittingthesky.net for more information.

We can organize to close the entire War on Terror torture gulag, not just Guantanamo—see www.cageprisoners.org and www.closegitmo.org.

We can start our own 9/11 truth groups (see www.911truth.org for a grassroots contact list) and join or contribute to one or more of the many professional organizations, including Architects and Engineers, Pilots, Veterans, Firefighters, Medical Professionals, Lawyers, and so on.

We can turn the U.S. towards a more balanced and peace-promoting position on the Palestine-Israel conflict by working with such organizations as www.vivapalestina-us.org, www.al-awda. com, www.freegaza.org, and www.jewishvoicesforpeace.org.

We can publicly confront lying politicians and media, videotape the encounters, and post the results on youtube. See www.wearechange.org.

We can *be the media* by: finding alternative stories or alternative spins at places like www.legitgov.org, www.whatreallyhappened. com, www.counterpunch.org, www.prisonplanet.com, www. globalresearch.ca, www.groups.yahoo.com/group/wvns/ and forwarding selected emails and urls to our friends, asking them to forward them to their friends, and so on; doing the same thing through Facebook, Twitter, and other networking tools; founding or joining truth-telling alternative newspapers such as the *Rock Creek Free Press* and the *Liberty Voice* (we can set up newsboxes in our communities to distribute these great papers; google and contact the publishers to find out how); starting our own local newsletters; listening to and informing our friends about truth-telling alternative radio networks such as American Freedom Radio, No Lies Radio, and others; volunteering for our local alternative newspapers and radio stations; getting involved with our local cable access channels and helping broadcast programming that questions the War on Terror (two good sources of such pro-

138 *How about Lyndon Larouche news magazine?*

gramming are www.911tv.org and www.911dvdproject.com);
distributing alternative DVDs such as those available for less than
50 cents each from www.911dvdproject.com; making our own
videos and putting them on youtube; making our own podcasts;
putting together micropower radio stations; and whatever else we
can dream up. Please note that broadcaster Dr. Hesham Tillawi
of www.currentissues.tv has offered to lend a hand to any would-
be broadcasters who want to challenge the Zionist-dominated
mainstream media on Middle East issues.

We can politely pressure our local public TV and radio
stations to broadcast programming that questions the War on
Terror. This can be done through emails, letters, and phone calls.
Recently Kyle Hence, producer of *9/11 Press for Truth*, worked
with KBDI-TV of Denver, Colorado to broadcast that film as a
fundraiser, and it was a huge success for the station. Contact Kyle
at www.911pressfortruth.com, or the makers of your favorite
alternative documentary, if you see an opening at your local public
TV station.

We can vote to ratify former Senator Mike Gravel's project
for national ballot initiatives, in a process patterned after the
Constitutional Conventions. This would give us a "plan B" for
when Congress doesn't represent us—as they don't on torture,
domestic spying, government secrecy, bailouts for the wealthiest,
perpetual wars and debt, ad nauseum. Get involved at www.vote.
org.

We can join the Continental Congress campaign to restore
Constitutional governance at www.wethepeoplefoundation.org.

We can pressure Congress to obey the Constitution and call
a long-overdue Article V Constitutional Convention: www.foavc.
org.

We can join together to oust all Congressional incumbents
(assuming they keep taking bribes and voting for the War on
Terror, banker bailouts, and other nonsense). Find out how at www.
firecongress.org.

We can end the private bankers' monopoly on the creation
of money, and return to a Constitutional currency that will help

bring peace and prosperity. Read the books and articles by Ellen Brown, Richard Cook, Geraldine Perry, G. Edward Griffin, and Umar Vadillo; visit www.communitycurrency.org; then contact Congress to support Dennis Kucinich's bill to nationalize the Fed, Ron Paul's bill to audit the Fed, and future bills to create a Constitutional currency.

We can grow the Transitions movement for a sustainable world by getting involved with local Transitions groups. Google "Transitions" and your state, city or region to find a local group.

We can call in to local talk shows and raise the issues discussed in this book.

We can attend local meetings where citizens' comments are allowed and raise the issues discussed in this book.

We can give away copies of this book to Obama voters we know, as well as to libraries, bookstores (discretely put it on the shelf to get it into the system), and our elected representatives. The publisher is offering ten copies for $50 plus postage to anyone who wants to give them away.

We can join together and hand out free food for peace—visit www.foodnotbombs.net.

We can become planetary citizens at www.thespiritualun.org.

We can get involved in a political party at the local, grassroots level and have an impact that is equivalent to many thousands of votes.

We can take President Obama at his word when he says "I want you to hold me accountable," by keeping track of how many promises he has kept, compromised, broken, or postponed, and then letting him know how we feel. Visit Obama's scorecard at www.politifact.com/truth-o-meter/promises/. As of this writing, Obama has kept thirty promises, compromised eight, broken six, and stalled on nine. Sixty-four are in the works, while he has taken no action on the vast majority of his promises—397 of them to be precise.

Obama would probably be happy if a citizen uprising forced him to bust the Bush regime, end the War on Terror, slash the military budget to save the economy, keep his promises and then some, and go down in history as the greatest president of all time. But he knows that, as JFK discovered, a president can only get so far out ahead of the people when taking on the military-industrial complex. He knows that for real change to occur, the people have to lead...*then* the leaders will follow.

Casting a vote is only the beginning. It's time for us to be the change we voted for.

Can we do it?

Yes we can.

References   SOURCES, CREDITS

1 Alex Lantier, "Obama announces escalation of war in Afghanistan, Pakistan," World Socialist Website (www.wsws.org/articles/2009/mar2009/afgh-m28.shtml).

2 "U.S. drone attack in Pakistan kills six villagers," Press TV, March 25, 2009 (www.presstv.com/detail.aspx?id=89590&sectionid=351020401).

3 Anwar Iqbal, "US to fight insurgency across Muslim world for 25 years" (www.atheonews.blogspot.com/2008/12/us-to-fight-insurgency-across-muslim.html).

4 "US troops may remain in Iraq in disguise after June 2009 withdrawal deadline," Thaindian News (www.thaindian.com/newsportal/world-news/us-troops-may-remain-in-iraq-in-disguise-after-june-2009-withdrawal-deadline_100133825.html).

5 Nasir Khan, "Will Obama Vacate Iraq?" *Dissident Voice* April 11, 2009 (www.dissidentvoice.org/2009/04/will-obama-vacate-iraq/).

6 Ibid.

7 John Basil Utley, "The Cost of Boots on the Ground in Iraq" (www.truthout.org/100108M).

8 Ibid.

9 David Usborne, "Obama pledges to protect CIA torture operatives" (www.independent.co.uk/news/world/americas/obama-pledges-to-protect-cia-torture-operatives-1670067.html).

10 Alex Spillius, "Barack Obama Discloses Bush Torture Methods Including Use of Insects," London *Telegraph*, 4/17/2009 (www.telegraph.co.uk/news/worldnews/northamerica/usa/barackobama/5167884/Barack-Obama-discloses-Bush-torture-methods-including-use-of-insects.html).

11 Mark Tran, "CIA Medics Joined in Guantanamo Torture Sessions, Says Red Cross," April 7, 2009 (www.guardian.co.uk/world/2009/apr/07/cia-medics-guantanamo-torture-red-cross).

12 Wayne Madsen Reports, May 29th-31st, 2009 (www.waynemadsenreports.com).

13 Glen Greenwald, " An emerging progressive consensus on Obama's executive power and secrecy abuses," Salon.com, 4/13/2009 (www.salon.com/opinion/greenwald/2009/04/13/obama/index.html).

14 "Obama's Military Budget: While media plays up program cuts, total defense budget surpasses Bush by $20 B," *Common Dreams* 4/9/2009 (www.commondreams.org/newswire/2009/04/09-8).

15 Steve Hargreaves, "'War on Terror' may cost $2.4 trillion: Congressional Budget Office expects the funds would keep 75,000 troops fighting in Iraq and Afghanistan for the next 10 years" (www.money.cnn.com/2007/10/24/news/economy/cbo_testimony/index.htm).

16 Vivien Lou Chen and Thomas Keene, "Economist Stiglitz Says Iraq War Costs May Reach $5 Trillion" (www.bloomberg.com/apps/news?pid=20601087&sid=acXcm.yk56Ko&refer=home).

17 From roughly 400 billion to 800 billion, so far, according to the Center on Budget and Policy Priorities (www.cbpp.org/cms/?fa=view&id=125).

18 www.realeconomy.com/

19 www.realeconomy.com/crime.htm

20 Deborah Davies, "Torture Inc. Americas Brutal Prisons" (www.informationclearinghouse.info/article8451.htm).

21 BBC, "US 'biggest global peace threat'" (www.news.bbc.co.uk/2/hi/americas/5077984.stm).

22 Ambrose Evans-Pritchard, "'Copper Standard' for the world's currency system?" The London *Telegraph*, 16 April 2009 (www.telegraph.co.uk/finance/comment/ambroseevans_pritchard/5160120/A-Copper-Standard-for-the-worlds-currency-system.html).

23 Tobacco Health Threat Dwarfs International Terrorism Deaths" (www.tobacco.org/news/215827.html). Medical errors, along with infections picked up in hospitals, kill between 100,000 and 200,000 people per year (American Iatrogenic Association: www.iatrogenic.org/). Automobiles kill about 42,000 Americans per year (www.driveandstayalive.com/info%20section/statistics/stats-usa.htm).

24 www.lightningsafety.com/nlsi_pls/probability.html (vs 3,000 terror deaths in 100 years = 30 per year).

25 National Safety Council (www.nsc.org/research/odds.aspx).

26 Robert Pape, *Dying to Win: The Strategic Logic of Suicide Terrorism* (NY: Random House, 2005) 4.

27 Ibid.

28 For an illustration of some of the difficulties of defining terrorism, see "Terrorism: The Problems of Definition," Center for Defense Information, August 1, 2003 (www.cdi.org/friendlyversion/printversion.cfm?documentID=1564).

29 Associated Press, "Poll: Iraqis support attacks on U.S. troops" (www.usatoday.com/news/washington/2006-09-27-iraqi-opinion_x.htm).

30 Military.com, "Afghan Support for NATO Troops Plummets" (www.military.com/news/article/February-2009/afghan-support-for-nato-troops-plummets.html).

31 www.jafi.org.il/education/hasbara/glossary.html

32 "Two thirds of the 621 children (two thirds under 15 years) killed at checkpoints, in the street, on the way to school, in their homes, died from small arms fire, directed in over half of cases to the head, neck and chest—the sniper's wound. Clearly, soldiers are routinely authorised to shoot to kill children in situations of minimal or no threat." Derek Summerfield, "Palestine: The Assault on Health and Other War Crimes," *British Medical Journal*, 10/16/04 (www.bmj.com/cgi/content/extract/329/7471/924).

33 Allen L. Roland, Ph.D., "The Death of Humanitarian Law Was Gaza" (www.blogs.salon.com/0002255/2009/04/28.html).

34 Reported by the Associated Press, archived at www.lawncafe.com/t5983-antiterror-funds-spent-on-lawn-mower-racing.html.

35 Melissa McNamara, CBS News, "Homeland Security Boondoggle: A Congressional Investigation Calls Into Question How Federal Money Is Being Spent" (www.cbsnews.com/stories/2007/03/01/cbsnews_investigates/main2529551.shtml).

36 Nafeez Ahmed, *The War on Truth: 9/11, Disinformation, and the Anatomy of Terrorism*. Ahmed's work on JCIT cites Philip Paull's MA thesis *"International Terrorism": The Propaganda War*, San Francisco State University, 1982.

37 Ibid.

38 Ibid.

39 www.historycommons.org/entity.jsp?entity=benjamin_netanyahu.

40 James Mann, *Rise of the Vulcans: The History of Bush's War Cabinet* (NY: Viking, 2004).

41 www.whatreallyhappened.com/fiveisraelis.html.

42 Reported in Haaretz April 16, 2008 (http://www.haaretz.com/hasen/spages/975574.html).

43 Shadia Drury, *Leo Strauss and the American Right* (NY: St. Martin's, 1997, 1999), 82.

44 Drury, 87.

45 Drury, 88.

46 Drury, 89.

47 "In the final analysis, Strauss's view of politics is much harsher and more radical than Schmitt's...Strauss's critique of Schmitt amounts to saying that Schmitt just does not go far enough." (Drury, 93).

144

48 Drury, 80.

49 Drury, 131.

50 Qtd. in Jim Lobe, "Strong Must Rule the Weak, said Neo-Cons' Muse," Inter Press News Agency, May 7, 2003 (ipsnews.net/interna.asp?idnews=18038).

51 Adolf Hitler, Mein Kampf, v. 1, ch. 10.

52 Drury, 81.

53 Drury, 81.

54 Drury, 119.

55 Bryan Sacks, "Making History: The Compromised 9/11 Commission." In Zarembka, ed. *The Hidden History of 9/11*. NY: Seven Stories, 2008 (Elsevier, 2006).

56 www.foreignaffairs.org/19981101faessay1434/ashton-b-carter-john-deutch-philip-zelikow/catastrophic-terrorism-tackling-the-new-danger.html

57 The Project for a New American Century, *Rebuilding America's Defenses: Strategy, Forces and Resources for a New Century* (www.newamericancentury.org), 51.

58 Robert Stinnett, *Day of Deceit* (NY: Free Press, 1999).

59 Brian Bogart, radio interview, "The Dynamic Duo," December 27, 2006 (www.gcnlive.com).

60 George Washington, *Farewell Address* (www.yale.edu/lawweb/avalon/washing.htm).

61 Joseph Gerson, *Empire and the Bomb: How the U.S. Uses Nuclear Weapons to Dominate the World* (London and Ann Arbor: Pluto Press, 2007).

62 William Blum, *Killing Hope: US Military and CIA Interventions Since World War II* (Monroe, ME: Common Courage Press, 2004).

63 Douglas Rushkoff, *Coercion* (NY: Penguin, 1999), 140.

64 Rushkoff, 141.

65 Lt. Col. Dave Grossman, *On Killing: The Psychological Cost of Learning to Kill in War and Society* (Boston, NY, Toronto, London: Little, Brown, 1995).

66 Zbigniew Brezezinksi, *The Grand Chessboard: American Primacy and its Geostrategic Imperatives* (NY: Penguin, 1997), 25.

67 Naomi Klein, *The Shock Doctrine: The Rise of Disaster Capitalism* (NY: Henry Holt and Company, 2007).

68 Brezezinski, 211.

69 www.hollywood.com/news/detail/id/311906

70 Jack Shaheen, *Reel Bad Arabs: How Hollywood Vilifies a People* (Northhampton, MA: Interlink, 2001).

71 Matthew Simmons, *Twilight in the Desert: The Coming Saudi Oil Shock and the World Economy* (Hoboken, NJ: 2005).

72 T.H. Meyer, *Reality, Truth, and Evil* (Forest Row, UK: Temple Lodge Publishing, 2005), 7.

73 Meyer, 68-69.

74 Meyer, 39.

75 Ibid.

76 David Griffin, *The New Pearl Harbor*, xi.

77 Niels H. Harrit, Jeffrey Farrer, Steven E. Jones, Kevin R. Ryan, Frank M. Legge, Daniel Farnsworth, Gregg Roberts, James R. Gourley, and Bradley R. Larsen, "Active Thermitic Material Discovered in Dust from the 9/11 World Trade Center Catastrophe," *The Open Chemical Physics Journal*, 2009, 2, 7-31 (www.bentham-open.org/pages/content.php?TOCPJ/2009/00000002/00000001/7TOCPJ.SGM).

78 Cited in Meyer, 38.

79 Cited in Meyer, 68.

80 On usury as the biggest weapon in the arsenal of empire, see John Perkins, *Confessions of an Economic Hit Man* (NY: Penguin 2004).

81 James Hider, "Iraq Prime Minister Nouri al-Maliki Demands US Withdrawal Timetable," *The Times* (UK) (www.timesonline.co.uk/tol/news/world/iraq/article4288108.ece)

82 Military.com, "Afghan Support for NATO Troops Plummets" (www.military.com/news/article/February-2009/afghan-support-for-nato-troops-plummets.html).

83 www.tvbgone.com

84 E.S. Herman, "Dasht-E Leili." www.zmag.org/sustainers/content/2004-04/07herman.cfm. Also see the documentary film *Afghan Massacre: The Convoy of Death* by Jamie Doran, www.moviesfoundonline.com/afghan_massacre.php.

85 ibid.

86 Duncan Campbell and Richard Norton-Taylor ,"U.S. accused of holding terror suspects on prison ships," *The Guardian,* June 2, 2008.

87 Moazzam Begg, *Enemy Combattant* (NY, London: The Free Press, 2006).

88 Grin, "Kids sodomized at Abu Ghraib, Pentagon has the videos - Hersh" (www.dailykos.com/story/2004/7/14/193750/666).

89 Alfred W. McCoy, *A Question of Torture: CIA Interrogation, from the Cold War to the War on Terror* (NY: Macmillan, 2006).

90 Alan Dershowitz, speech at Jewish Community Center in Creve Coeur, Missouri. Cited in Kurt Nimmo, "Alan Dershowitz and the Ticking Time Bomb" (www.informationclearinghouse.info/article1842.htm).

91 In *Coercion: Why We Listen to What "They" Say* (NY: Penguin/Putnam, 2002) Douglas Rushkoff explains that torture and other techniques of coercion are about exerting control, not finding truth.

92 Jonathan S. Landay and Warren P. Strobel, "Cheney's speech ignored some inconvenient truths," McClatchy Newspapers, May 21, 2009 (www.mcclatchydc.com/226/story/68643.html).

93 Sen. Carl Levin, D-MI, declassified version of Senate Armed Services Committee's Report on its investigation into the treatment of detainees in U.S. custody, April 21, 2009, quoted www.huffingtonpost.com/sen-carl-levin/new-report-bush-officials_b_189823.html.

94 Jonathan S. Landay, "Report: Abusive tactics used to seek Iraq-al Qaida link," McClatchy Newspapers, April 21, 2009 (www.mcclatchydc.com/227/story/66622.html?ref=fp1).

95 Ben Macintyre, "'24' is fictional. So is the idea that torture works," *The Times* April 23, 2009 (www.timesonline.co.uk/tol/comment/columnists/ben_macintyre/article6150151.ece).

96 Naomi Klein, *The Shock Doctrine*, chapter 1 (NY: Henry Holt and Company, 2007).

97 FBI sources say Abu Zubaida "is largely a loudmouthed and mentally troubled hotelier whose credibility dropped as the CIA subjected him to a simulated drowning technique known as waterboarding and to other 'enhanced interrogation' measures." Dan Eggen and Walter Pincus, "FBI, CIA Debate Significance of Terror Suspect, Agencies Also Disagree On Interrogation Methods," Washington *Post*, December 17, 2007 (www.washingtonpost.com/wp-dyn/content/article/2007/12/17/AR2007121702151.html).

98 Robert Baer, "The CIA's Gift to Conspiracy Theorists," *Time* magazine, December 7, 2007.

99 Ibid.

100 "Robert Baer Says Evidence Points To 911 Inside Job," PrisonPlanet.com (www.prisonplanet.com/articles/november2007/031107Baer.htm).

101 Marjorie Cohn, "Aggressive War: Supreme International Crime," November 9, 2004 (www.web.archive.org/web/20041110060613/www.truthout.org/docs_04/110904A.shtml).

102 Gilbert Burnham, Riyadh Lafta, Shannon Doocy, and Les Roberts. "Mortality after the 2003 invasion of Iraq: a cross-sectional cluster sample survey." *The Lancet*, 11 October 2006. This study found that by 2006 the number of Iraqis killed by the war had reached 655,000. By extrapolation, the Iraq body count alone reached one million by 2008. ———

103 Michelle Nichols, "Muslims believe U.S. goal to weaken Islam: poll," Reuters, April 24, 2007 (www.reuters.com/article/politicsNews/idUSN2332112320070424?feedType=RSS).

104 John Vinocur, "Politicus: Bush might be heading for tangle with neocons," International Herald Tribune, January 11, 2005.

105 Bernard Lewis, "The Roots of Muslim Rage," *The Atlantic*, September 1990 (www.theatlantic.com/doc/199009/muslim-rage).

106 Edward Said, "Impossible Histories: Why the Many Islams Cannot Be Simplified." *Harpers*, July 2002, 71.

107 Samuel Huntington, "The Clash of Civilizations." *Foreign Affairs*, v72, n3, Summer 1993 (www.alamut.com/subj/economics/misc/clash.html).

108 Ibid.

109 Ibid.

110 Patrick J. Buchanan, *The Death of the West* (NY: St. Martin's, 2002) 118.

111 *The Coming Religious Wars? Demographics and Conflict in Islam and Christianity.* Pew Research Center forum, Washington, DC (www.pewforum.org/events/?EventID=82).

112 Spengler, "The demographics of radical Islam." *Asia Times,* August 23, 2005 (www.atimes.com/atimes/Front_Page/GH23Aa01.html).

113 Patrick Rael, "Do they really hate freedom? The myth of the insane terrorist." *The Bowdoin Orient,* April 15, 2005 (www.orient.bowdoin.edu/orient/article.php?date=2005-04-15&id=2&section=2).

114 "Bin Laden says he wasn't behind attacks." *CNN* report, September 17, 2001 (www.archives.cnn.com/2001/US/09/16/inv.binladen.denial/).

115 Interview with Osama Bin Laden. *Ummat* (Pakistan), September 28, 2001. Archived at www.public-action.com/911/oblintrv.html.

116 "FBI says, 'No Hard Evidence Connecting Bin Laden to 9/11.'" Originally published by *The Muckraker Report*, June 6, 2006, and *Ithaca Journal*, June 29, 2006. Judged as one of the top censored stories of the year by *Project Censored* and archived at www.projectcensored.org/top-stories/articles/16-no-hard-evidence-connecting-bin-laden-to-9-11/.

117 "News of Bin Laden's Death and Funeral 10 days ago." al-Wafd (Egypt), Wednesday, December 26, 2001 Vol 15 No 4633. Archived along with many other reports of Bin Laden's death at whatreallyhappened.com/WRHARTICLES/osama_dead.html.

118 Bruce Lawrence, ed., James Howarth, trans., *Messages To The World: The Statements of Osama Bin Laden* (London: Verso, 2005). Lawrence is quoted in an ABC news report casting doubt on the authenticity of an alleged Bin Laden tape and suggesting that Bin Laden was long dead: "Duke Professor Skeptical of bin Laden Tape" (www.abclocal.go.com/wtvd/story?section=news/local&id=3828678). Lawrence stated in a radio interview with the author (February 16th, 2007, www.gcnlive.com) that he had come to believe that Bin Laden had been dead for some time, and that many of the alleged Bin Laden videos were fake. Lawrence also stated in the radio interview that the alleged "confession video" presented by the US government

in December, 2001 is "bogus" and that all of his many acquaintances in the CIA Bin Laden detail know it is bogus.

119 Ed Haas, "FBI says, 'No hard evidence connecting Bin Laden to 9/11'" (www. muckrakerreport.com/id267.html).

120 Rael.

121 Ibid.

122 Ed Haas, "FBI says, 'No hard evidence connecting Bin Laden to 9/11.'"

123 www.fbi.gov/wanted/topten/fugitives/laden.htm

124 "Bush rejects Taliban offer to hand Bin Laden over," *The Guardian*, October 14, 2001. www.guardian.co.uk/world/2001/oct/14/afghanistan.terrorism5.

125 "Diplomats Met With Taliban on Bin Laden, Some Contend U.S. Missed Its Chance," *The Washington Post* October 29, 2001. Archived at www.infowars.com/saved%20pages/Prior_Knowledge/U.S._met_taliban.htm.

126 "Bush rejects Taliban offer to hand Bin Laden over," *The Guardian*, October 14, 2001.

127 Ed Haas, "FBI says, 'No hard evidence connecting Bin Laden to 9/11.'"

128 London *Times*, July 22nd 2002, qtd. in Paul Thompson, *The Terror Timeline: Year by Year, Day by Day, Minute by Minute: A Comprehensive Chronicle of the Road to 9/11—and America's Response*. This evidence is summarized in Nafeez Ahmed, *The War on Truth: 9/11, Disinformation, and the Anatomy of Terrorism* Northampton, Mass.: Interlink, 2005) 147-153, and David Griffin, *The New Pearl Harbor*, 105-108.

129 Ibid.

130 Drew Brown, "Tora Bora a lost victory," *Knight Ridder Tribune*, October 20, 2002 (web.archive.org/web/20030804035648/www.tallahassee.com/mld/tallahassee/news/nation/4324811.htm). Referenced at www.historycommons.org/timeline.jsp?complete_911_timeline__war_on_terrorism__outside_iraq=escapeFromAfghanistan&timeline=complete_911_timeline.

131 *Christian Science Monitor*, March 4, 2002 and other newspapers, cited in Thompson.

132 *London Telegraph*, February 23, 2002.

133 *Newsweek*, August 11, 2002.

134 White House press conference, March 13, 2002 (www.whitehouse.gov/news/releases/_2002/03/20020313-8.html).

135 CNN Evans, Novak, Hunt & Shields, "Interview With General Richard Myers," Aired April 6, 2002 (www.transcripts.cnn.com/TRANSCRIPTS/0204/06/en.00.html).

136 *London Daily Mirror*, July 8, 2002 (cited in www.complete911timeline.org/entity.jsp?entity=mullah_omar).

137 *New Yorker*, October 16, 2001 (cited in www.complete911timeline.org/entity.jsp?entity=mullah_omar).

138 An impressive selection of mainstream news stories and other well-sourced entries concerning the history of the Afghanistan pipeline project is available at www.historycommons.org/timeline.jsp?timeline=complete_911_timeline&before_9/11=pipelinePolitics.

139 Karl Schwartz, "Phew! Bush Dirty Diapers!" (www.rense.com/general82/dite.htm).

140 Jean-Charles Brisard and Guillaume Dasquie, *Bin Laden: The Forbidden Truth* (NY: Nation Books, 2002) 43.

141 George Arney, "U.S. 'Planned Attack on Taleban'" (BBC, September 18, 2001).

142 Qtd. in Salim Muwakkil, "Pipeline Politics Taint U.S. War," *Chicago Tribune*, March 18, 2002.

: JOE KLEIN Pg. —

: Leo StrausS

Creator of The Noble Lie

head of Office of Special Plans :

143 M K Bhadrakumar, "Russia takes control of Turkmen (world?) gas," *Asia Times*, July 30, 2008 (www.atimes.com/atimes/Central_Asia/JG30Ag01.html).

144 Karl Schwartz, "We Are At The Edge Of The Abyss" (www.rense.com/general82/abyss.htm).

145 Karen De Young, "Afghanistan Opium Crop Sets Record, U.S.-Backed Efforts At Eradication Fail," *Washington Post* December 2, 2006 (www.washingtonpost.com/wp-dyn/content/article/2006/12/01/AR2006120101654.html).

146 Mike Ruppert, *Crossing the Rubicon: The Decline of the American Empire at the End of the Age of Oil* (Gabriola Island, BC: New Society Publishers, 2004), 58. Rupert cites a range of estimates for drug and money laundering figures circa 1999-2000, and argues the best estimate is 600 billion and 1.5 trillion dollars per year respectively.

147 Ruppert, 68.

148 Ibid.

149 De Young.

150 Bob Considine, "Author claims White House knew Iraq had no WMD: Journalist Ron Suskind says Bush ordered forgery linking Saddam, al-Qaeda," MSNBC August 5, 2008 (www.msnbc.msn.com/id/26030573/).

151 www.downingstreetmemo.com/memos.html

152 Considine.

153 www.sourcewatch.org/index.php?title=Taking_the_fight_to_the_terrorists

154 Ibid.

155 Kissinger's authorship of "Seizing Arab Oil" is discussed in Robert Dreyfuss, "The Thirty-Year Itch: For Three Decades, Washington's Hawks Have Pushed for the United States to Seize Control of the Persian Gulf. Their Time Is Now," *Mother Jones*, March/April 2003, 41-45. See also: www.polytropos.org/2004/01/23/seizing-arab-oil/.

156 Eigen's Political and Historical Quotations (www.politicalquotes.org/Quotedisplay.aspx?DocID=57359). Imagine someone saying "Money is much too important a commodity to be left in the hands of the Jews." Would such a bigot be tolerated? So why hasn't Kissinger's quote gotten him universally reviled as a racist and bigot?

157 Melanie Gosling, "'U.S. Invasion of Iraq Was a Resource War,'" *Cape Times*, South Africa, May 4, 2005 (archived at www.commondreams.org/headlines05/0504-06.htm).

158 www.allacademic.com/meta/p21288_index.html (presented August, 2005).

159 "Some claim Iraqi oil potential is enormous: Iraq has 'more crude oil' than Saudi Arabia" (www.energyinvestmentstrategies.com/2008/03/02/some-claim-iraqi-oil-potential-is-enormous/).

160 Matt Simmons, *Twilight in the Desert: The Coming Saudi Oil Shock and the World Economy*. Hoboken, NJ: John Wiley and Sons, 2005.

161 James Kunstler, *The Long Emergency*.

162 Ron Susskind, *The Price of Loyalty: George W. Bush, the White House, and the Education of Paul O'Neill* (NY: Simon and Schuster, 2004) 86.

163 Ibid. 96.

164 Ibid.

165 Ibid.

166 Jason Leopold, " The Secret Deal For Iraq's Oil" (www.uruknet.de/?p=m46494&hd=&size=1&l=e). Sourced to "The Public Record" (www.pubrecord.org/nationworld/262.html?task=view).

167 Antonia Juhasz and Raed Jarrar, "Oil Grab in Iraq," *Foreign Policy in Focus*, February 22, 2007 (www.fpif.org/fpiftxt/4020).

A Grand Chessboard War

168 Naomi Klein, "Big Oil's Iraq deals are the greatest stick-up in history: The country's invaders should be paying billions in reparations not using the war as a reason to pillage its richest resource," *The Guardian*, July 4, 2008 (www.guardian. co.uk/commentisfree/2008/jul/04/oil.oilandgascompanies).

169 Ibid.

170 Ibid.

171 Cyrus Bina, "Economist Devastates 'War for Oil' Dogma" (www.atheonews. blogspot.com/2008/12/economist-devastates-war-for-oil-dogma.html).

172 James Petras, "Zion-power and War: From Iraq to Iran. The Deadly Embrace" (www.petras.lahaine.org/articulo.php?p=1713&more=1&c=1).

173 www.whatreallyhappened.com/fiveisraelis.html

174 Robert G. Kaiser, "Bush and Sharon Nearly Identical On Mideast Policy," *Washington Post*, February 9, 2003 (www.washingtonpost.com/ac2/wp-dyn?pagenam e=article&node=&contentId=A45652-2003Feb8&notFound=true)

175 Emad Mekay, " IRAQ: War Launched to Protect Israel - Bush Adviser," IPS, March 29, 2004 (www.ipsnews.net/interna.asp?idnews=23083).

176 James Petras, *The Power of Israel in the United States* (Atlanta: Clarity Press, 2006).

177 James Petras, statement on *Dynamic Duo* radio show, March 28, 2008 (www. gcnlive.com).

178 www.time-blog.com/swampland/2008/06/neocons_gone_wild.html

179 Ray McGovern, former President's Daily Briefer for the CIA, discusses the fact that Israel is not a U.S. ally, and the reasons why Israel refused formal alliance with the U.S., in Dahr Jamail, "Interview With Ray McGovern, Part 2" (dahrjamailiraq.com/ hard_news/archives/newscommentary/000459.php).

180 *Associated Press*, "Poll Says Most Americans Believe Saddam-9/11 Link Has Been Proven," July 23, 2003 (archived at www.commondreams.org/headlines03/0701-05. htm).

181 Angus Reid Global Monitor, "Polls & Research: Some Americans Still Link Hussein to 9/11," September 9, 2006 (www.angus-reid.com/polls/view/13081).

182 The only conceivable exception might be cases of hot pursuit, where the pursuing government agent has personally witnessed criminal behavior and is in the process of attempting to apprehend the criminal, *and* where failing to intrude on someone's privacy would cause an immediate, specific and grave danger. If there is no actual hot pursuit, *or* there is no grave danger to be averted, then the Fourth Amendment restrictions must apply.

183 Andrew Harris, "Spy Agency Sought U.S. Call Records Before 9/11, Lawyers Say," *Bloomberg.com*, June 30 2006 (www.bloomberg.com/apps/news?pid=2060108 7&sid=abIV0cO64zJE&refer).

184 Vyan, "Operation FirstFruits : NSA spied on Dissenters and Journalists?" (www. dailykos.com/story/2006/1/19/14619/9977).

185 Nick Langewis and David Edwards, "Constitutional expert: FISA bill 'is an evisceration of the Fourth Amendment,'" *The Raw Story* June 19 2008 (rawstory.com/ news/2008/Turley_FISA_bill_is_evisceration_of_0619.html)

186 Nat Hentoff, "No Place to Hide. National Security Agency, not the Times, greatly harms our constitutional privacy," *The Village Voice*, January 10, 2006 (www. villagevoice.com/2006-01-10/news/no-place-to-hide/).

187 Ibid.

188 Paul Thompson, *The Terror Timeline: Year by Year, Day by Day, Minute by Minute* (NY: Harper Collins, 2004). On-line version at www.historycommons.org/project. jsp?project=911_project.

189 CNN: "Ex-CIA director: U.S. faces 'World War IV.'" April 3, 2003 (www.cnn.com/2003/US/04/03/sprj.irq.woolsey.world.war/index.html).

190 Ibid.

191 Pape, 4.

192 en.wikipedia.org/wiki/Gunpowder_Plot (accessed 8/23/2008).

193 Qtd. in Barrie Zwicker, *Towers of Deception: The Media Coverup of 9/11* (Gabriola Island, BC: New Society Publishers, 2006) 258.

194 Webster Tarpley, *9/11 Synthetic Terror: Made in USA* (Joshua Tree, CA: Progressive Press, 2005) 68.

195 en.wikipedia.org/wiki/Remember_the_Maine (accessed 8/24/08).

196 John K. Winkler, *William Randolph Hearst: A New Appraisal* (NY: Hastings, 1955), 95. Some consider the quote apocryphal, including W. Joseph Campbell in "Not likely sent: The Remington-Hearst 'telegrams.'" Journalism and Mass Communication Quarterly (summer 2000), academic2.american.edu/~wjc/wjc3/notlikely.htm.

197 The 1964 *Warren Report* concluded that "Oswald acted alone," while the 1978 House Assassinations Investigation concluded that JFK had died as the result of a conspiracy that probably involved elements of organized crime.

198 David Ruppe, "U.S. Military Wanted to Provoke War With Cuba. Book: Military Drafted Plans to Terrorize U.S. Cities to Provoke War With Cuba," ABC News, May 1, 2001 (abcnews.go.com/US/story?id=92662).

199 James Bamford, *Body of Secrets* (NY: Doubleday, 2001).

200 Ibid.

201 www.archives.gov/research/jfk/search.html

202 James Douglas, *JFK and the Unspeakable: Why He Died and Why It Matters* (Orbis: Maryknoll, NY, 2008). See also E. Martin Schotz, *History Will Not Absolve Us* (Kurz, Ulmer, & DeLucia, Brookline, MA, 1996).

203 John M. Newman , *JFK and Vietnam: Deception, Intrigue, and the Struggle for Power* (NY: Warner Books, 1992). Newman's evidence, and Chomsky's astonishingly weak argument against its obvious implications for the JFK assassination, is discussed in Michael Morrissey, *Looking for the Enemy* (Lulu.com, 1993, 2007).

204 Ganser, Daniele: *NATO's Secret Armies. Operation Gladio and Terrorism in Western Europe* (London: Frank Cass, 2005).

205 Daniele Ganser, "NATO's Secret Armies Linked to Terrorism?" *Global Research*, December 17, 2004 (www.globalresearch.ca/articles/GAN412A.html).

206 Ibid.

207 Ibid.

208 Ibid.

209 Illan Pappé, *The Ethnic Cleansing of Palestine* (London and NY: Oneworld, 2006).

210 Ostrovsky, Victor and Hoy, Claire: *By Way of Deception* (NY: St. Martin's, 1991).

211 "Israel honors 9 Egyptian spies. After 50 years, President Katsav presents three surviving members with certificates of appreciation at Jerusalem ceremony," Reuters, March 30 2005 (www.ynetnews.com/Ext/Comp/ArticleLayout/CdaArticlePrintPrevie w/1,2506,L-3065838,00.html#n, accessed August 31 2008).

212 My main source on the U.S.S. *Liberty* is James Bamford, *Body of Secrets* (NY: Doubleday, 2001).

213 Peter Hounem, *Operation Cyanide: Why the Bombing of the USS Liberty Nearly Caused World War III* (London: Satin Publications, 2003).

214 Qtd. in Hounem, 68.

215 Hounem, 69.

216 Photographs of the letters may be viewed at www.yenra.com/anthrax-letters-pictures/.

217 "Anthrax suspect passed 2 polygraphs: Handwriting analysis also failed to tie Ivins to letters," World Net Daily, August 7, 2009 (www.wnd.com/index.php?fa=PAGE.view&pageId=71721). *(handwritten star)*

218 Ibid.

219 Stephen Kiehl and Josh Mitchell, "Doubts Persist on Ivins' Guilt: Scientists and Legal Experts Skeptical," The Baltimore Sun, August 8, 2008 (www.baltimoresun.com/news/nation/bal-te.anthrax08aug08,0,427841.story).

220 John Byrne, "Anthrax spores don't match dead researcher's samples," February 26, 2009 (www.rawstory.com/news/2008/Anthrax_spores_dont_match_dead_researchers_0226.html).

221 Jack Dolan and Dave Altimari, "Anthrax Missing From Army Lab," Hartford Courant, Jan, 20, 2002 (archived at www.whatreallyhappened.com/ARCHIVE/ctnow_com%20SPECIALS.htm).

222 Laura Rozen, "Fort Detrick's Anthrax Mystery" (www.dir.salon.com/story/news/feature/2002/01/26/assaad/index.html).

223 Barbara Honegger, "The Scarlet A" (www.truthjihad.com/scarlet.htm).

224 Ibid.

225 Anthony York, "Why Daschle and Leahy? It's the question no one in Washington or the media wants to publicly examine: Why were two high-profile Democrats targeted by the anthrax mail terrorist?" Salon.com, November 12, 2001 (www.archive.salon.com/politics/feature/2001/11/21/anthrax/index.html). *(handwritten star)*

226 David Ray Griffin, The New Pearl Harbor: Disturbing Questions About the Bush Administration, 2nd edition (Northampton, MA: Interlink, 2004) 195.

227 www.911independentcommission.org/questions.html

228 CBC News, August 21, 2006, www.cbc.ca/sunday/911hamilton.html.

229 www.911review.com/coverup/commission.html.

230 Sonny Bunch, "Debunking 9/11: It's time to finally put the conspiracy theories to rest," The Weekly Standard, September 11, 2006 (www.weeklystandard.com/Content/Public/Articles/000/000/012/665awcva.asp?pg=1)

231 CBC News, August 21, 2006, www.cbc.ca/sunday/911hamilton.html.

232 To find the professional organizations, Google "engineers 9/11 truth," "firefighters 9/11 truth," "lawyers 9/11 truth," and so on. *(handwritten: a real name?)*

233 For a list of suggested readings by these researchers, see Appendix A.

234 NewsMax, "Louis Freeh Charges 9/11 Commission Cover-Up." November 17, 2005 (www.archive.newsmax.com/archives/articles/2005/11/17/122900.shtml). *(handwritten star)*

235 www.securingamerica.com/node/692

236 Cited in Alan Miller, "Twenty-five U.S. Military Officers Challenge Official Account of 9/11" (www.opednews.com/articles/genera_alan_mil_080112_twenty_five_u_s__mil.htm).

237 Robert Baer, "The CIA's Gift to Conspiracy Theorists," Time Magazine, (www.time.com/time/nation/article/0,8599,1692518,00.html).

238 Cited in Griffin, The New Pearl Harbor Revisited, xx.

239 Pre-publication edition of John Farmer, The Ground Truth: The Story Behind America's Defense on 9/11 (NY: Houghton Mifflin, scheduled for publication fall 2009), cited at www.prisonplanet.com/911-commission-counsel-government-agreed-to-lie-about-911.html.

240 Griffin summarizes the lies of the 9/11 Commission in "The 9/11 Commission Report: A 571-Page Lie" (www.911truth.org/article.php?story=20050523112738404)

241 9/11 Commission Report, 172.

242 Griffin, "The 9/11 Commission Report A 571-Page Lie."

243 Kolar.

244 Griffin, *The New Pearl Harbor* 67; reported in *Washington Post*, May 17, 2002.

245 Ibid. 68.

246 "Tom Clancy Novels Foretell a 9/11-Like Attack and a Post-9/11 World" (www.911blogger.com/node/14694).

247 "The Lone Gunmen: Pilot episode of X-Files spin off an insider 911 warning or sick conditioning?" (www.prisonplanet.com/multimedia priorknowledge lonegumen.html). Footage from this episode is included in the documentary *Core of Corruption*.

248 Ibid. 68-69; Griffin, *The New Pearl Harbor Revisited* 134.

249 Ibid. 68.

250 Paul Zarembka, "Initiation of the 9/11 Operation, with Evidence of Insider Trading," in *The Hidden History of 9/11* 47-74.

251 *9/11 Commission Report*, 172 (note).

252 *9/11 Commission Report*, 172.

253 Sander Hicks, *The Big Wedding* (NY: Vox Pop, 2006) 13.

254 Ibid.

255 Alex Jones show, October 10, 2001, cited in Griffin, *The New Pearl Harbor* 84.

256 William Norman Grigg, "Did We Know What Was Coming?" *New American* magazine, March 11, 2002, cited in Nafeez Ahmed *The War on Truth* 110, and Griffin, *The New Pearl Harbor* 85.

257 "Bin Laden says he wasn't behind attacks." *CNN* report, September 17 2001 (archives.cnn.com/2001/US/09/16/inv.binladen.denial/).

258 Interview with Osama Bin Laden. *Ummat* (Pakistan), September 28, 2001. Archived at www.public-action.com/911/oblintrv.html.

259 "FBI says, 'No Hard Evidence Connecting Bin Laden to 9/11.'" Originally published by *The Muckraker Report*, June 6, 2006, and *Ithaca Journal*, June 29, 2006. Judged as one of the top censored stories of the year by *Project Censored* and archived at www.projectcensored.org/top-stories/articles/16-no-hard-evidence-connecting-bin-laden-to-9-11/.

260 "U.S. RELEASES VIDEOTAPE OF OSAMA BIN LADEN." Official U.S. government press release. Archived and discussed in Edward F. Haas, "Osama bin Laden 'confession video' unplugged" (www.muckrakerreport.com/id301.html).

261 *9/11 Commission Report*, 50.

262 Ibid. 160, 154. Cited in David Ray Griffin, "Was America Attacked by Muslims on 9/11?" (www.davidraygriffin.com/articles/was-america-attacked-by-muslims-on-911/).

263 "A Careful Sequence of Mundane Dealings Sows a Day of Bloody Terror for Hijackers," *The Wall Street Journal*, October 16, 2001 (www.cooperativeresearch.org/timeline/2001/wallstreetjournal101601.html). Cited in Yasmin Ahmed, "The Remaking of Islam in the Post 911 Era" (in Barrett, Cobb, and Lubarsky, *9/11 and American Empire* v.2).

264 Kevin Fagan, "Agents of Terror Leave Their Mark on Sin City," San Francisco Chron-icle, October 4, 2001 (www.sfgate.com/cgi-bin/article.cgi?file=/chronicle/archive/2001/10/04/MN102970.DTL). Cited in Griffin, "Was America Attacked by Muslims on 9/11?"

265 www.cooperativeresearch.org/context.jsp?item=a091101beforepinkpony

266 Murphy, Shelly and Belkin, Douglas. "Hijackers Said to Seek Prostitutes," Boston Globe, October 10, 2001. Cited in Yasmin Ahmed.

267 Bailey, Eric. "It Was A Little Strange. Most People Want To Do Take-Offs And Landings. All They Did Was Turns," *The Daily Mail,* September 16, 2001. Cited in Yasmin Ahmed.

268 www.davidraygriffin.com/articles/was-america-attacked-by-muslims-on-911/

269 Questions about the apparent lack of response by U.S. air defenses on 9/11 were first raised on the internet by Jared Israel and others, and summarized in Nafeez Ahmed, *The War on Truth* (Joshua Tree, CA: Progressive Press, 2002) chapter 5, 144-175; and David Ray Griffin, *The New Pearl Harbor* Part One 3-64. These questions have been masterfully elucidated in subsequent works by Dr. Griffin including *The 9/11 Commission Report: Omissions and Distortions* Part Two 137-275; *Debunking 9/11 Debunking* 27-94; *9/11 Contradictions* 80-139; and *The New Pearl Harbor Revisited,* 1-128.

270 Griffin, *The New Pearl Harbor Revisited* (Northhampton, MA: Interlink, 2008) 1-2.

271 Dr. Robert Bowman, a fighter pilot and former head of the US military's space weapons program under presidents Ford and Carter, has repeatedly asserted that "had standard operating procedures been followed, the planes would not have reached their targets." Dr. Bowman has confirmed that the description offered here of how common intercepts are, and how quickly they happen, is at least roughly accurate based on his extensive knowledge of military procedures involving fighter planes (personal communication, December 16, 2007).

272 Bowman, the former head of the U.S. military's space weapons program, states: "I'm an old interceptor ... If our government had done nothing that day, and let normal procedure be followed, those planes, whatever they were, would have been intercepted." *9/11 and the Neocon Agenda* conference, Los Angeles, California, June 2006.

273 *The New Pearl Harbor,* 7.

274 Griffin deconstructs the military's contradictory stories in the works cited in note 4, especially *The 9/11 Commission Report: Omissions and Distortions* Part Two 137-275.

275 Dean Jackson, dnotice.org, *Rock Creek Free Press,* August 2008.

276 Thierry Meyssan, *9/11: The Big Lie* (London: Carnot, 2002) 18. Meyssan cites White House and Andrews Air Force Base documents showing that recently-revamped air defenses included five batteries of anti-aircraft missiles atop the Pentagon as well as two fighter squadrons on permanent alert at Andrews Air Force Base. He also told David Ray Griffin that French and Saudi officers confirmed that they had seen these anti-missile batteries during tours of the Pentagon, and Griffin found other testimony supporting the existence of the batteries, as reported in *The New Pearl Harbor Revisited,* 106-107.

277 Mark Gaffney, *The 9/11 Mystery Plane and the Vanishing of America* (NY: Trineday, 2008).

278 A.K. Dewdney, "Project Achilles Report," 4/19/2003 (www.physics911.net/projectachilles).

279 *9/11 Commission Report* 31.3, cited in Griffin, *9/11 Contradictions,* 80.

280 FAA sources contradicting the military-9/11 Commission version include a 2003 FAA memo to the 9/11 Commission, other FAA statements, and statements by FAA public relations representative Laura Brown. See Griffin, *9/11 Contradictions* 80-139.

281 Jackson, ibid.

282 Griffin, *The New Pearl Harbor Revisited,* 90.

283 The contradictions between official story #2 and official story #3, both of which were offered under oath to the 9/11 Commission by top military personnel, are summarized in Griffin, *9/11 Contradictions* 80-139.

284 Questions raised by Bush's actions on 9/11 have been discussed in Gore Vidal, *Dreaming War: Blood for Oil and the Cheney-Bush Junta* (NY: Thunder's Mouth Press/Nation Books, 2002) 11-56; Griffin, *The New Pearl Harbor* 57-64; and Webster Tarpley, *9/11: Synthetic Terror* (Joshua Tree, CA: Progressive Press, 2005) 272-310.

285 Richard Gage, AIA, "Blueprint for Truth," video (www.ae911truth.org).

286 David Ray Griffin, "The Destruction of the World Trade Center: Why the Official Account Cannot Be True" 80-94. In Paul Zarembka, ed. *The Hidden History of 9/11: Second Edition* (NY: Seven Stories Press, 2008). Originally published in 2006 by JAI Press, an imprint of Elsevier, Europe's leading academic publishing house. While my discussion is indebted to Dr. Griffin's work, I have not reproduced it verbatim; those who want to read Dr. Griffin's argument firsthand should consult his essay. Note that I have elided two of his points, the production of dust and the production of dust clouds, and added a new one, demolition rings and squibs.

287 www.patriotsquestion911.com/engineers.html#Jowenko

288 Architects and Engineers for 9/11 Truth (www.ae911truth.org).

289 James Glanz, A Nation Challenged: The Site; Engineers Have a Culprit in the Strange Collapse of 7 World Trade Center: Diesel Fuel," *The New York Times,* November 29, 2001 (www.nytimes.com/2001/11/29/nyregion/nation-challenged-site-engineers-have-culprit-strange-collapse-7-world-trade.html?sec=&spon=&pagewanted=all).

290 Jim Hoffman, "The North Tower's Dust Cloud: Analysis of Energy Requirements for the Expansion of the Dust Cloud Following the Collapse of 1 World Trade Center" (www.911research.wtc7.net/papers/dustvolume/volumev4.html).

291 Cited in David Ray Griffin, "The Destruction of the World Trade Center: Why the Official Account Cannot Be True" (www.911review.com/articles/griffin/nyc1.html).

292 Kevin Ryan, " 9/11: Looking for Truth in Credentials: The Peculiar WTC 'Experts,'" *Global Research*, March 13, 2007 (www.globalresearch.ca/index.php?context=viewArticle&code=RYA20070313&articleId=5071).

293 Kevin Ryan, "Looking for Truth in Credentials: The WTC 'Experts'" (www.911blogger.com/node/6765).

294 Ibid.

295 Ibid.

296 Griffin, *The 9/11 Commission Report: Omissions and Distortions*.

297 Ryan.

298 www.wecanchangetheworld.wordpress.com/2008/09/01/dr-fr-greening-responds-to-nists-report-on-wtc-7/

299 Niels H. Harrit, Jeffrey Farrer, Steven E. Jones, Kevin R. Ryan, Frank M. Legge, Daniel Farnsworth, Gregg Roberts, James R. Gourley, and Bradley R. Larsen, "Active Thermitic Material Discovered in Dust from the 9/11 World Trade Center Catastrophe," *The Open Chemical Physics Journal*, 2009, 2, 7-31 (www.bentham-open.org/pages/content.php?TOCPJ/2009/00000002/00000001/7TOCPJ.SGM).

300 Elaine Jarvik, "Traces of explosives in 9/11 dust, scientists say," *Deseret News*, April 6, 2009 (www.deseretnews.com/article/0,5143,705295677,00.html).

301 *The New Pearl Harbor* 176.

302 *America Rebuilds*, PBS documentary, 2002. In 2005, reacting to 9/11 skeptics who had been harping on this quote for almost three years, the U.S. State Department cited a Silverstein PR spokesperson claiming that "pull it" meant pulling firemen out of the building. The many problems with this interpretation include: The fact that there were no firemen in Building 7 during the afternoon of 9/11; the fact that Silverstein has admitted that he made the statement in the afternoon, when no firemen were in the building ("We Are Change Confronts Larry Silverstein 3/13/08," www.911blogger.com/node/14361); and the juxtaposition "made that decision to pull *and we watched*

What about the two people in Bldg. #7 one who has mysteriously died, ?

the building collapse" suggesting that the decision and the collapse happened in fairly quick succession, with an implied causal relationship between the decision and the collapse.

303 Griffin, *The New Pearl Harbor Revisited* 56.

304 www.historycommons.org/entity.jsp?entity=larry_silverstein

305 Ibid.

306 Ibid.

307 Ibid.

308 Ibid.

309 Ibid.

310 Ibid.

311 Anemona Hartocollis, "Developer Sues to Win $12.3 Billion in 9/11 Attack," *New York Times,* March 27, 2008 (www.nytimes.com/2008/03/27/nyregion/27rebuild.html).

312 " Asbestos use in Construction," (www.asbestos.com/world-trade-center/asbestos.php).

313 "The Trouble with WTC Asbestos," May 5, 2008 (www.joecrubaugh.com/blog/2008/05/05/the-trouble-with-wtc-asbestos/).

314 Douglas McCleod, "Port loses claim for asbestos removal," (www.allbusiness.com/legal/trial-procedure-judges/9160294-1.html).

315 Eric Huffschmidt, *Painful Questions: An Analysis of the September 11th Attack* (Goleta, CA: Endpoint, 2002) 92.

316 Paulo Lima, "Five Men Detained as Suspected Conspirators," Bergen, New Jersey *Record*, September 12, 2001, cited in Justin Raimondo, *The Terror Enigma* (NY: iUniverse, 2003) xi.

317 ABC News, "The White Van: Were Israelis Detained on Sept. 11 Spies?" June 22, 2002, archived at www.commondreams.org/headlines02/0622-05.htm.

318 Ibid.

319 Ibid.

320 Ibid.

321 Cameron's report was taken down from the Fox website less than a week after it was posted. It is archived at www.100777.com/usa/israeli_spyring.

322 PBS *Newshour*, December 11, 2002 (www.pbs.org/newshour/bb/congress/july-dec02/intelligence_12-11.html).

323 Sylvain Cypel, "An Enigma: Vast Israeli Spy Network Dismantled in the US," *Le Monde*,

March 5, 2002, tr. Malcolm Garris, archived at www.antiwar.com/rep/lemonde1.html.

324 Christopher Ketcham, "The Israeli 'Art Student" Mystery," *Salon.com*, May 7, 2002 (dir.salon.com/story/news/feature/2002/05/07/students/index.html). On the close proximity of Mossad agents and alleged 9/11 terrorists, see also Mathias Gebauer, "Mossad Agents Were on Atta's Heels," *Der Spiegel*, October 1, 2002, cited in Raimondo 46.

325 Ibid.

326 Yuval Dror, "Odigo says workers were warned of attack," *Haaretz*, September 26, 2001 (www.haaretz.com/hasen/pages/ShArt.jhtml?itemNo=77744).

327 Ruppert 257.

328 Ibid. 259.

329 Michael Andregg, *Rethinking 9/11: Why Truth and Reconciliation Are Better Strategies than Global War* (www.gzmn.org/).

[handwritten note: Atta supposedly on Jack Abramhoff's yacht]

330 "Filmmaker Michael Moore Now Says 9/11 Could Be Inside Job" (www.infowars.com/articles/sept11/moore_911_could_be_inside_job.htm).

33 www.transcripts.cnn.com/TRANSCRIPTS/0605/20/tt.01.html

332 Thierry Meyssan, *L'Effroyable Imposture*, in English as *9/11 The Big Lie* (London: Carnot, 2002).

333 Jon Henley, "U.S. Invented Air Attack on Pentagon, Claims French Book." *The Guardian,* April 2, 2002 (www.guardian.co.uk/international/story/0,3604,677083,00.html).

334 Al-Jazeera, *Al-Ittija' al-mu'aqis* with host Dr. Faisal al-Qasim and guest Thierry Meyssan, October, 2003.

335 www.judicialwatch.org/5772.shtml

336 "Pandora's Black Box," video documentary (www.pilotsfor911truth.org).

337 www.thepentacon.com

338 April Gallop interview, Truth Jihad Radio, American Freedom Radio network, April 11, 2009, archived at www.americanfreedomradio.com/Barrett_09.html. Gallop stated in a private telephone conversation after the interview that she has been in contact with many of her fellow Pentagon victims and witnesses, none of whom saw any evidence of an airliner crash.

339 Barbara Honegger, "The Pentagon Attack Papers" (www.blog.lege.net/content/Seven_Hours_in_September.pdf).

340 George Nelson, Colonel, USAF (ret.), "911 - Aircraft Parts As A Clue To Their Identity: The Precautionary Principle" (www.rense.com/general64/prec.htm).

341 "Pandora's Black Box (www.pilotsfor911truth.org).

342 Ibid.

343 Ibid.

344 Dave Lindorff, "9/11: Missing Black Boxes in World Trade Center Attacks Found by Firefighters, Analyzed by NTSB, Concealed by FBI," *Counterpunch,* December 16, 2005 (www.counterpunch.org/lindorff12202005.html).

345 Ibid.

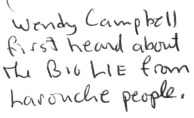

how about the 50 + video camera tapes focused on the Pentagon?

how about the Pentagon clocks mystery?

Wendy Campbell first heard about the BIG LIE from Larouche people.

How about the Israelis caught in the Mexican Parliment Bldg, ī armaments ???? Late 2001(?)

ABOUT THE AUTHOR

Kevin Barrett holds a Ph.D. in African Languages and Literature (Arabic-Islamic Studies focus) from the University of Wisconsin-Madison.

In 2006 a group of Republican politicians, led by State Representative Steve Nass, led an unsuccessful campaign to have him fired from his teaching post at the University of Wisconsin-Madison due to his public questioning of the War on Terror and the official account of 9/11.

Dr. Barrett was turned down for a tenure-track teaching job at the University of Wisconsin-Whitewater for purely political reasons even though he was the most qualified finalist, and finally the only candidate after the other two finalists went elsewhere, according to then-Dean of Humanities Dr. Howard Ross.

Since 2007 he has been effectively blacklisted by the University of Wisconsin-Madison and other American universities. Barred from his chosen profession for his political views, Dr. Barrett has worked as a nonprofit organizer, author, lecturer, talk radio host, and candidate for the U.S. House of Representatives. His website is www.truthjihad.com.